POE...
PLEASURE

BOOK I

POEMS FOR PLEASURE

CHOSEN AND EDITED BY

A. F. SCOTT

BOOK I

CAMBRIDGE
AT THE UNIVERSITY PRESS
1955

Published by the Syndics of the Cambridge University Press
Bentley House, 200 Euston Road, London NW1 2DB
American Branch: 32 East 57th Street, New York, N.Y.10022

ISBN 0 521 06244 6

First published 1955
Reprinted 1956 1959 1961
1964 1966 1969 1972

Printed in Great Britain
at the University Printing House, Cambridge
(Brooke Crutchley, University Printer)

CONTENTS

PART I

§1. RHYTHM IN VERSE

CONTENTS

§2. PICTURES IN WORDS

§3. TALES AND MINSTRELSY

CONTENTS

§4. THE POET'S FEELING

PART II

§1. THE POET'S SONG

CONTENTS

§2. THE NATURAL SCENE

§3. BALLADS OLD AND NEW

CONTENTS

§4. THE POET'S HEART

INTRODUCTION

It has been said that boys and girls in the secondary school do not like poetry. This perhaps unexpected statement is supported by the evidence of many teachers today. Poetry, they say, cannot compete in attractiveness with music; and in immediacy of appeal painting is far more popular. In the English lesson, prose stories, plays, composition work are all considered to be more interesting and enjoyable than poetry.

This is remarkable, because from the nursery onwards children show a real delight in rhythm and the merry jingle of words. They enjoy nursery rhymes, and like games turning on these rhymes, sing-songing them throughout the house or in the open air. They like phrases that have the touch of poetry about them: namby-pamby, fiddle-faddle, higgledy-piggledy. And the language of poetry so often resembles the language of children, being fresh and imaginative.

Perhaps one reason why boys in the secondary school do not like poetry is that now they are trying to master prose: not only to read it with understanding but to write it. Prose is the medium used for all subjects now being studied—history, geography, science, as well as English. The most important activity, therefore, is to understand the meaning whatever the particular subject may be. Meaning is all important.

It would therefore appear that schoolboys do not like poetry because they cannot always understand it. They look first of all for a meaning, feeling that now they should understand and are exasperated when they do not. When the meaning of a line or of a verse of poetry is carefully explained to them they wonder why the poet could not say whatever he had to say more simply, or even why he did not say it in prose. Some teachers, moreover, stress the importance of meaning too much, so that a poem becomes material for translation from one set of words into another, and the class may well find the translation the more satisfactory!

Yet boys and girls still enjoy the sound of words and the rhythm of phrases, and take an eager delight in music. They are fond of singing and dancing, perhaps even more than when they were younger. They enjoy drawing and painting, and making illustrations for the stories they have read. And they are fascinated by prose stories, by narratives of action. They are now beginning to respond more fully to the emotions they see expressed in films, pantomimes, and plays.

One may, I think, appeal to the capacity to enjoy all these things in presenting poetry. When we consider the simplest elements of poetry we see that a poem consists of a tune, a picture, a story, and a feeling. Though these are closely related, fused together into a single artistic whole, yet it is possible to select poems which will show each particular element above the rest. Poems can be chosen with a very strongly marked rhythm, where sound is more important than the other elements—as in nonsense verse, some early folk-songs, sea shanties, marching songs. Here meaning is of little or no importance. Such poetry may be enjoyed for the sound alone, for the exhilaration the words can give, spoken singly or in chorus, whispered, shouted aloud, moving sometimes as fast as a galloping horse, and sometimes as slowly as a ceremonial procession.

Then a poem can be a picture in words. The young have powers of vivid visualization. Let them read such poems to see trees and birds and animals, the world around them, described with a new clarity and precision. Let them draw what they are now looking at through the eyes of the poet, and so find a new delight in the poet's power to describe. They will enjoy this keener sight, and begin to see things more vividly themselves.

Once schoolboys can appreciate the narrative skill of the old ballads, in close relationship perhaps to the narrative technique of the cinema, they may be moved and excited by the economy, imagination and energy of these tales, and may find ballads and their modern counterparts better than some of the prose narratives they are accustomed to.

Finally, they may be presented with suitable poems expressing the poet's feelings of joy or of unhappiness, and such emotions as anger, grief or pity, which are within their own normal experience and so embodying the important factor of recognition. They may well respond to these expressions of feeling, and later come to appreciate poems revealing the more profound thoughts and emotions.

In his book, *Poetry in School*, Dr J. H. Jagger recalls an eminent lecturer who when instructing his audience of teachers in training said that a poem 'could be studied for the facts it contained, or for its formal characteristics, or for the meaning of the words, or for their derivation, or for its moral (if it contained a perceptible moral), or for its allusions (if there were any), or it could be treated as an historical document (if it had any value of that kind), or it could be correlated with some other subject of instruction, or it could be used as a grammatical exercise, or it could be compared with a standard—given marks, so to speak—or it could be committed to memory'.

Today, our attitude to poetry in schools is mercifully more enlightened, though some of these methods of 'teaching' poetry are still to be found in the class-room. You may notice that though the catalogue above is pretty exhaustive it omits one prime feature (an omission which utterly condemns all the rest) —enjoyment of poetry for its own sake. Wordsworth said that poetry is written to give pleasure.

This selection of poems has been made with this one end constantly in view. They are poems for pleasure, carefully chosen first to recapture the boy's delight in rhythm and picture, in story and feeling, and then leading him progressively to enjoy these four aspects of poetry and to what may be a more complete enjoyment of their summed effect than would otherwise be possible.

The anthology is divided into four parts, one for each school year in the secondary school, and each part is divided into four sections. Introducing each section are brief commentaries on one aspect of poetry under the four main groupings—and each commentary enlarges on what is said in the corresponding commentary in the preceding part. So there is a continuity from one part to the next, and a unity in each individual part.

The anthology covers the first four years in the secondary school. The poems have not only been especially chosen to suit the age and interests of the pupil, but have been carefully arranged by subject so that they bear a close relationship to other poems in the section. This arrangement throws similarities (and sometimes differences) of expression and treatment into strong relief, and gives additional point to the anthology as a whole.

About half the poems are by modern poets, showing that poetry is not something unrelated to modern life, a collection of museum pieces, but a natural and instinctive expression of the human spirit, as much alive and as vital today as in the past.

A. F. SCOTT

June 1954

ACKNOWLEDGMENTS

I should like to acknowledge my deep personal debt to Mr C. E. Carrington for his friendly encouragement and expert advice over a number of years, and especially for his most valued guidance in the compiling of this Anthology. I wish also to express my thanks to the staff of the Cambridge University Press for their patience and continued help.

The author's thanks are due to the following for permission to quote copyright matter:

Mr Walter de la Mare and Messrs Faber & Faber (*The Linnet, Off the Ground, The Little Creature, Silver, The Pool in the Rock, Nicholas Nye*); Dr John Masefield, O.M., the Society of Authors and the Macmillan Company, New York (*Sea Fever* and *The Rider at the Gate*); The Clarendon Press, Oxford (*I love all beauteous things* and *Spring Goeth all in White*, taken from *The Shorter Poems of Robert Bridges*); Mrs W. B. Yeats and Messrs Macmillan & Co., Ltd. (*Lake Isle of Innisfree* and *The Fiddler of Dooney* from *Collected Poems of W. B. Yeats*); Mr Ralph Hodgson and Messrs Macmillan & Co., Ltd. (*The Bells of Heaven* and *Stupidity Street* from *Poems*); the Hardy Estate and Messrs Macmillan & Co., Ltd. (*The Darkling Thrush* and *Weathers* from *Collected Poems of Thomas Hardy*); Mrs G. Bambridge, Messrs Macmillan & Co., Ltd. and the Macmillan Company of Canada (*Heriot's Ford* by Rudyard Kipling from *Songs from Books*); Mrs Edward Thomas and Messrs Faber & Faber (*Tall Nettles, The Hollow Wood* and *Adlestrop*); Mr Robert Graves (*Flying Crooked* from *Collected Poems 1914–1947* published by Messrs Cassell & Co., Ltd.); Mrs Harold Monro (*Milk for the Cat* and *Overheard on a Saltmarsh*); The Macmillan Company, New York (*Daniel* and *The Congo* from the *Collected Poems of Vachel Lindsay*); Mrs W. H. Davies and Messrs Jonathan Cape, Ltd. (*The Kingfisher* and *A Great Time* from *The Collected Poems of W. H. Davies*); Mrs James Stephens and Messrs Macmillan & Co., Ltd. (*The Fifteen Acres*, *The Snare* and *The Shell* from *The Collected Poems of James Stephens*); Miss D. E. Collins and Messrs Methuen & Co., Ltd. (*The Song of Quoodle* from *The Collected Poems of G. K. Chesterton*); Sir John Squire (*There was an Indian*); Messrs Sidgwick & Jackson (*The Soldier* and *The Great Lover* from *The Collected Poems of Rupert Brooke*; *Blackbird* and *Moonlit Apples* from *Poems* by John Drinkwater; *Ducks* by F. W. Harvey; and *The Volunteer* from *Poems* by H. Asquith); Messrs Gerald Duckworth & Co., Ltd. (*The South Country* by Hilaire Belloc from *Sonnets and Verse*); Messrs A. D. Peters (*The End of the Road* by Hilaire Belloc); Mrs Frieda Lawrence and Messrs William Heinemann, Ltd. (*Bat* and *Snake* by D. H. Lawrence); Messrs Faber & Faber (*O What is that Sound* by W. H. Auden from *Collected Shorter Poems 1930–44*); the Rev. Dr Andrew Young and Messrs Jonathan Cape, Ltd. (*The Eagle* from *The Collected Poems of Andrew Young*); Dr O. St J. Gogarty and Messrs Constable & Co., Ltd. (*Croker of Ballinagarde*); Mr Charles Dalmon and Messrs Constable & Co., Ltd. (*O What if the Fowler*); Mr Padraic Colum, the Talbot Press, Dublin, and Devin-Adair Co., New York (*Old Woman of the Roads*); Mr J. B. Morton (*The Dancing Cabman* from *By the Way*); Mr A. C. Benson and Messrs John Lane (*The Hawk*); Messrs Longmans, Green & Co., Ltd. (*The Dromedary* from *Poems* by A. Y. Campbell); Messrs Curtis Brown, Ltd. (*Horses on the Carmargue* by Roy Campbell from *Adamastor* published by Messrs Faber & Faber); Mr Edmund Blunden (*The Pike* and *The Poor Man's Pig*); Mr Rex Warner and Messrs John Lane (*Lapwing* and *Mallard* from *Poems and Contradictions*); Mr C. Day Lewis and Hogarth Press, Ltd.

ACKNOWLEDGMENTS

(*You that love England*); Oxford University Press (*Pied Beauty* and *The Woodlark* from *The Poems of Gerard Manley Hopkins*); Lloyds Bank, Ltd. as Executor of the late Mrs Sylvia Lynd (*The Flycatcher*); Messrs Martin, Secker & Warburg (*Miss Thompson Goes Shopping* by Martin Armstrong).

A. F. SCOTT

SCHEME OF BOOK II

PART III

[TUNE]

1. The Magic of Words

Words have not only sound and meaning but associations. Consideration of words 'horse', 'charger', 'steed'; associations of words 'castle', and 'treasure'. The flavour of words—poets' inventions. The magic of sound in a passage full of Proper Names.

[PICTURE]

2. The Poet's Vision

The significance of Spring among primitive people. Myths in which Nature is as real as a living thing. Greek and Roman mythology. Gods and goddesses referred to as though living persons. Personification in poetry. Extension in metaphor. Poets' images revealing a keener vision of the world.

[STORY]

3. Narrative Poems on Sea and Land

Primitive men were hunters and warriors. One of the tribe relates stories of their successful exploits. Beginning of narrative poetry—stories usually founded on fact, dealing with battles on sea and land, hunting and action. Similar subjects treated by poets.

[FEELING]

4. The Poet and the Modern World

World of nature to primitive man peopled with spirits. Tried to establish harmony of human culture with natural environment. All now changed—world of machines. Complete revolution in living—machines hated at first—then accepted, sometimes personified. Have not yet brought the golden age.

Index of Authors

PART IV

1. The Music of Poetry

The regular rhythm of feet of savages became in time feet of poetic metre. Metre a mechanical pattern. Variety of such patterns—stressed and unstressed syllables. Alliteration, rhyme, assonance, a poem scanned—iambuses, trochees, anapaests, dactyls. Effect of music of poetry.

2. Scenes of the Machine Age

The tradition of nature poetry. Now a changed world. New technique in description—experiment and invention. Romance in modern poetry. The adaptation for present poetic needs.

3. Stories of Pure Imagination

Reverie, free association and day-dreaming. Day-dreams shaped and controlled. The importance of the imagination. Romantic poetry. 'The willing suspension of disbelief.' The range of such romantic poetry.

4. The Eternal Theme

Feelings and their association with values. The highest ideals—supreme values—beauty, truth and goodness. Poetry and these supreme values. Thoughts on life and death. How can we enjoy a sad poem? Poem not mere statement of loss but work of art. Its power to expand in the mind, giving pleasure.

Index of First Lines

xix

PART I

RHYTHM IN VERSE

We love the movement of running, skipping, jumping. We enjoy still more the flowing movement of dancing. Our instinctive enjoyment of dancing is much the same as that of savages with their rhythmical tribal dance round the camp fire. The feet of the savages keep time to the beating of native drums and the men call and shout with excitement. As they dance and cry out they make a kind of magic spell to bring them success as hunters and warriors. From this early magic, and from this rhythmic dancing, poetry was born.

We have much the same response to rhythm ourselves. We are brought up to the sound of nursery rhymes such as:

> Hey diddle diddle
> The cat and the fiddle
> The cow jumped over the moon.

Nursery rhymes have a pleasing rhythm coming from a jumble of words which might very well be a magic spell, for we cannot understand exactly what some of the words and phrases mean.

The rhythm of the sound of words has not only been pleasing and exciting; it has had other uses. It has helped men in pulling on the oar, pushing the capstan, or hauling up the sails in such vigorous sea shanties as the one beginning:

> Blow the man down bullies
> Blow the man down.

It has helped in the swing of the march:

> Kentish Sir Byng stood for his King
> Bidding the cropheaded Parliament swing

And, pressing a troop unable to stoop
And see the rogues flourish and honest folk droop
Marched them along, fifty score strong,
Great-hearted gentlemen, singing this song.

And can't you feel the left, right, left, right of a marching column of men in these lines:

Don't-don't-don't-don't-look at what's in front of you
(Boots-boots-boots-boots-movin' up and down again)
Men-men-men-men-men go mad with watchin' 'em
An' there's no discharge in the war!

Though we may not sing a song in time to our work today (we do have 'music while you work' in factories), we carry in our heads all kinds of jingles because the rhythm is so pleasing:

Eena, meena, mina, mo.
Yankee doodle dandy.

We delight in the use of words imitating sounds:

quack-quack, cuckoo, clink, clank, sizzle, murmur, splash.

and in phrases and sentences such as:

Higgledy, piggledy.
I'm the king of the castle.
Pop goes the weasel.

All these—nursery rhymes, shanties, marching songs, proverbs, catch-phrases, slogans—charm and please us because they have lilt and rhythm.

Rhythm is the first and most important element of poetry.

Sail Hauling

Blow the man down, bullies
Blow the man down!
Way, hey; blow the man down.
Blow him right down from the top of his crown!
Give us a chance to blow the man down.

4

Piping

The piper came to our town,
To our town, to our town,
The piper came to our town,
And he played bonnily,
And wasn't he a roguey
A roguey, a roguey,
And wasn't he a roguey
The piper of Dundee?

Girls and Boys, come out to play

Girls and boys, come out to play,
The moon is shining bright as day;
Leave your supper and leave your sleep
And come with your playfellows into the street;
Come with a WHOOP, and come with a call,
Come with a good will, or come not at all;
Up the ladder and down the wall
A half-penny roll will cover us all.
You find milk and I'll find flour,
And we'll have a pudding in half-an-hour.

Come, Lasses and Lads

Come, lasses and lads, get leave from your dads,
  And away to the maypole hie,
For every fair has a sweetheart there,
  And the fiddler's standing by;

For Willy shall dance with Jane,
And Johnny has got his Joan,
To trip it, trip it, trip it, trip it,
Trip it up and down.

Now there they did stay the whole of the day,
  And tired the fiddler quite
With dance and play, without any pay,
  From morning unto night.

5

They told the fiddler then
They'd pay him for his play,
And each a two-pence, two-pence, two-pence
Gave him and went away.

My Mother said

My mother said, I never should
Play with the gypsies in the wood.

If I did, then she would say:
'Naughty girl to disobey!

'Your hair shan't curl and your shoes shan't shine,
You gypsy girl, you shan't be mine!'

And my father said that if I did,
He'd rap my head with the teapot-lid.

My mother said that I never should
Play with the gypsies in the wood.

The wood was dark, the grass was green;
By came Sally with a tambourine.

I went to sea—no ship to get across;
I paid ten shillings for a blind white horse.

I upped on his back and was off in a crack,
Sally tell my mother I shall never come back.

Widdicombe Fair

'Tom Pearce, Tom Pearce, lend me your grey mare,'
  (All along, down along, out along, lee.)
'For I want for to go to Widdicombe Fair,
  Wi' Bill Brewer, Jan Stewer, Peter Gurney, Peter Davy,
    Dan'l Whiddon, Harry Hawk,
  Old Uncle Tom Cobbley and all,
    Old Uncle Tom Cobbley and all.'

'And when shall I see again my grey mare?'
  (All along, down along, out along, lee.)
'By Friday soon, or Saturday noon,
  Wi' Bill Brewer, Jan Stewer, Peter Gurney, Peter Davy,
    Dan'l Whiddon, Harry Hawk,
  Old Uncle Tom Cobbley and all,
    Old Uncle Tom Cobbley and all.'

Then Friday came, and Saturday noon,
  (All along, down along, out along, lee.)
But Tom Pearce's old mare hath not trotted home,
  Wi' Bill Brewer, Jan Stewer, Peter Gurney, Peter Davy,
    Dan'l Whiddon, Harry Hawk,
  Old Uncle Tom Cobbley and all,
    Old Uncle Tom Cobbley and all.

So Tom Pearce he got up to the top o' the hill,
  (All along, down along, out along, lee.)
And he seed his old mare down a-making her will,
  Wi' Bill Brewer, Jan Stewer, Peter Gurney, Peter Davy,
    Dan'l Whiddon, Harry Hawk,
  Old Uncle Tom Cobbley and all,
    Old Uncle Tom Cobbley and all.

So Tom Pearce's old mare her took sick and her died,
  (All along, down along, out along, lee.)
And Tom he sat down on a stone, and he cried,
  Wi' Bill Brewer, Jan Stewer, Peter Gurney, Peter Davy,
    Dan'l Whiddon, Harry Hawk,
  Old Uncle Tom Cobbley and all,
    Old Uncle Tom Cobbley and all.

But this isn't the end o' this shocking affair,
  (All along, down along, out along, lee.)
Nor, though they be dead, of the horrid career
  Of Bill Brewer, Jan Stewer, Peter Gurney, Peter Davy,
    Dan'l Whiddon, Harry Hawk,
  Old Uncle Tom Cobbley and all,
    Old Uncle Tom Cobbley and all.

7

When the wind whistles cold on the moor of a night,
   (All along, down along, out along, lee.)
Tom Pearce's old mare doth appear, ghastly white,
    Wi' Bill Brewer, Jan Stewer, Peter Gurney, Peter Davy,
    Dan'l Whiddon, Harry Hawk,
   Old Uncle Tom Cobbley and all,
     Old Uncle Tom Cobbley and all.

And all the night long be heard skirling and groans,
   (All along, down along, out along, lee.)
From Tom Pearce's old mare in her rattling bones,
    And from Bill Brewer, Jan Stewer, Peter Gurney, Peter Davy,
    Dan'l Whiddon, Harry Hawk,
   Old Uncle Tom Cobbley and all,
     Old Uncle Tom Cobbley and all.

Off the Ground

Three jolly Farmers
Once bet a pound
Each dance the others would
Off the ground.
Out of their coats
They slipped right soon,
And neat and nicesome
Put each his shoon.
One—Two—Three!
And away they go,
Not too fast
And not too slow;
Out from the elm-tree's
Noonday shadow,
Into the sun
And across the meadow.
Past the schoolroom,
With knees well bent,
Fingers a-flicking,
They dancing went.

Upsides and over,
And round and round,
They crossed click-clacking
The Parish bound;
By Tupman's meadow
They did their mile,
Tee-to-tum
On a three-barred stile.
Then straight through Whipham
Downhill to Week,
Footing it lightsome
But not too quick,
Up fields to Watchet
And on through Wye,
Till seven fine churches
They'd seen skip by—
Seven fine churches,
And five old mills,
Farms in the valley,
And sheep on the hills;
Old Man's Acre
And Dead Man's Pool
All left behind
As they danced through Wool.
And Wool gone by
Like tops that seem
To spin in sleep
They danced in dream:
Withy—Wellover—
Wassop—Wo—
Like an old clock
Their heels did go.
A league and a league
And a league they went,
And not one weary
And not one spent.
And lo! and behold!
Past Willow-cum-Leigh

9

Stretched with its waters
The great green sea.
Says Farmer Bates:
'I puffs and I blows,
What's under the water
Why no man knows!'
Says Farmer Giles:
'My mind comes weak,
And a good man drownded
Is far to seek.'
But Farmer Turvey,
On twirling toes,
Ups with his gaiters,
And in he goes:
Down where the mermaids
Pluck and play
On their twangling harps
In a sea-green day;
Down where the mermaids,
Finned and fair,
Sleek with their combs
Their yellow hair...
Bates and Giles
On the shingle sat,
Gazing at Turvey's
Floating hat.
But never a ripple
Nor bubble told
Where he was supping
Off plates of gold.
Never an echo
Rilled through the sea
Of the feasting and dancing
And minstrelsy.
They called—called—called:
Came no reply:
Nought but the ripples'
Sandy sigh.

Then glum and silent
They sat instead
Vacantly brooding
On home and bed,
Till both together
Stood up and said:
'Us knows not, dreams not
Where you be,
Turvey, unless
In the deep blue sea;
But axcusing silver—
And it comes most willing—
Here's us two paying
Our forty shilling;
For it's sartin sure, Turvey,
Safe and sound
You danced us square, Turvey,
Off the ground!'   WALTER DE LA MARE

The Dancing Cabman

Alone on the lawn
    The cabman dances;
In the dew of dawn
    He kicks and prances.
His bowler is set
    On his bullet head,
For his boots are wet,
    And his aunt is dead.
There on the lawn
    As the light advances,
On the tide of the dawn
    The cabman dances.

Swift and strong
    As a garden roller,
He dances along
    In his little bowler,

Skimming the lawn
　　With royal grace,
The dew of the dawn
　　On his great red face.
To fairy flutes,
　　As the light advances,
In square black boots
　　The cabman dances.　　J. B. MORTON

The End of the Road

In these boots and with this staff
Two hundred leaguers and a half
Walked I, went I, paced I, tripped I,
Marched I, held I, skelped I, slipped I,
Pushed I, panted, swung and dashed I;
Picked I, forded, swam and splashed I,
Strolled I, climbed I, crawled and scrambled,
Dropped and dipped I, ranged and rambled;
Plodded I, hobbled I, trudged and tramped I,
And in lonely spinnies camped I,
Lingered, loitered, limped and crept I,
Clambered, halted, stepped and leapt I,
Slowly sauntered, roundly strode I,
And...
Let me not conceal it...rode I.

(For who but critics could complain
Of 'riding' in a railway train?)

Across the valleys and the high land,
With all the world on either hand,
Drinking when I had a mind to,
Singing when I felt inclined to;
Nor ever turned my face to home
Till I had slaked my heart at Rome.
　　　　　　　　　　　HILAIRE BELLOC

The Owl

When cats run home and light is come,
  And dew is cold upon the ground,
And the far-off stream is dumb,
  And the whirring sail goes round,
  And the whirring sail goes round;
    Alone and warming his five wits,
    The white owl in the belfry sits.

When merry milkmaids click the latch,
  And rarely smells the new-mown hay,
And the cock hath sung beneath the thatch
  Twice or thrice his roundelay,
  Twice or thrice his roundelay;
    Alone and warming his five wits,
    The white owl in the belfry sits.

LORD TENNYSON

The Owl and the Pussy-Cat

The Owl and the Pussy-Cat went to sea
  In a beautiful pea-green boat,
They took some honey, and plenty of money,
  Wrapped up in a five-pound note.
The Owl looked up to the stars above,
  And sang to a small guitar,
'O lovely Pussy! O Pussy, my love,
  What a beautiful Pussy you are,
    You are,
    You are!
  What a beautiful Pussy you are!'

Pussy said to the Owl, 'You elegant fowl!
  How charmingly sweet you sing!
O let us be married! too long we have tarried
  But what shall we do for a ring?'

They sailed away for a year and a day,
  To the land where the Bong-tree grows,
And there in a wood a Piggy-wig stood,
  With a ring at the end of his nose,
    His nose,
    His nose,
  With a ring at the end of his nose.

'Dear Pig, are you willing to sell for one shilling
  Your ring?' Said the Piggy, 'I will.'
So they took it away, and were married next day
  By the Turkey who lives on the hill.
They dined on mince, and slices of quince,
  Which they ate with a runcible spoon;
And hand in hand, on the edge of the sand,
  They danced by the light of the moon,
    The moon,
    The moon,
  They danced by the light of the moon.

EDWARD LEAR

The Pobble who has no Toes

The Pobble who has no toes
  Had once as many as we;
When they said, 'Some day you may lose them all;'
  He replied,—'Fish fiddle de-dee!'
And his Aunt Jobiska made him drink,
Lavender water tinged with pink,
For she said, 'The World in general knows
There's nothing so good for a Pobble's toes!'

The Pobble who has no toes,
  Swam across the Bristol Channel;
But before he set out he wrapped his nose
  In a piece of scarlet flannel.
For his Aunt Jobiska said, 'No harm
Can come to his toes if his nose is warm;
And it's perfectly known that a Pobble's toes
Are safe,—provided he minds his nose.'

The Pobble swam fast and well,
  And when boats or ships came near him
He tinkledy-blinkledy-winkled a bell,
  So that all the world could hear him.
And all the Sailors and Admirals cried,
When they saw him nearing the further side,—
'He has gone to fish, for his Aunt Jobiska's
Runcible Cat with crimson whiskers!'

But before he touched the shore,
  The shore of the Bristol Channel,
A sea-green Porpoise carried away
  His wrapper of scarlet flannel.
And when he came to observe his feet,
Formerly garnished with toes so neat,
His face at once became forlorn
On perceiving that all his toes were gone!

And nobody ever knew
  From that dark day to the present,
Whoso had taken the Pobble's toes,
  In a manner so far from pleasant.
Whether the shrimps or crawfish gray,
Or crafty Mermaids stole them away—
Nobody knew; and nobody knows
How the Pobble was robbed of his twice five toes!

The Pobble who has no toes
  Was placed in a friendly Bark,
And they rowed him back, and carried him up,
  To his Aunt Jobiska's Park.
And she made him a feast at his earnest wish
Of eggs and buttercups fried with fish;—
And she said,—'It's a fact the whole world knows,
That Pobbles are happier without their toes.'

EDWARD LEAR

The Jumblies

They went to sea in a Sieve, they did,
  In a Sieve they went to sea:
In spite of all their friends could say,
On a winter's morn, on a stormy day,
  In a Sieve they went to sea!
And when the Sieve turned round and round,
And every one cried, 'You'll all be drowned!'
They called aloud, 'Our Sieve ain't big,
But we don't care a button! we don't care a fig!
  In a Sieve we'll go to sea!'
    Far and few, far and few,
      Are the lands where the Jumblies live;
      Their heads are green, and their hands are blue,
      And they went to sea in a Sieve.

They sailed away in a Sieve, they did,
  In a Sieve they sailed so fast,
With only a beautiful pea-green veil
Tied with a riband by way of a sail,
  To a small tobacco-pipe mast;
And every one said, who saw them go,
'O won't they be soon upset, you know!
For the sky is dark, and the voyage is long,
And happen what may, it's extremely wrong
  In a Sieve to sail so fast!'
    Far and few, far and few,
      Are the lands where the Jumblies live;
      Their heads are green, and their hands are blue,
      And they went to sea in a Sieve.

The water it soon came in, it did,
  The water it soon came in;
So to keep them dry, they wrapped their feet
In a pinky paper all folded neat,
  And they fastened it down with a pin.
And they passed the night in a crockery-jar,
And each of them said, 'How wise we are!

Though the sky be dark, and the voyage be long,
Yet we never can think we were rash or wrong,
  While round in our Sieve we spin!'
    Far and few, far and few,
      Are the lands where the Jumblies live;
     Their heads are green, and their hands are blue,
     And they went to sea in a Sieve.

And all night long they sailed away;
  And when the sun went down,
They whistled and warbled a moony song
To the echoing sound of a coppery gong,
  In the shade of the mountains brown.
'O Timballo! How happy we are,
When we live in a sieve and a crockery-jar,
And all night long in the moonlight pale,
We sail away with a pea-green sail,
  In the shade of the mountains brown!'
    Far and few, far and few,
      Are the lands where the Jumblies live;
     Their heads are green, and their hands are blue,
     And they went to sea in a Sieve.

They sailed to the Western Sea, they did,
  To a land all covered with trees,
And they bought an Owl, and a useful Cart,
And a pound of Rice and a Cranberry Tart,
  And a hive of silvery Bees.
And they bought a Pig, and some green Jackdaws,
And a lovely Monkey with lollipop paws,
And forty bottles of Ring-Bo-Ree,
  And no end of Stilton Cheese.
    Far and few, far and few,
      Are the lands where the Jumblies live;
     Their heads are green and their hands are blue,
     And they went to sea in a Sieve.

And in twenty years they all came back,
  In twenty years or more,
And everyone said, 'How tall they've grown!

For they've been to the Lakes, and the Terrible Zone,
  And the hills of the Chankly Bore';
And they drank their health, and gave them a feast
Of dumplings made of beautiful yeast;
And everyone said, 'If we only live,
We too will go to sea in a Sieve,—
  To the hills of the Chankly Bore!'
    Far and few, far and few,
      Are the lands where the Jumblies live;
      Their heads are green, and their hands are blue,
      And they went to sea in a Sieve.

EDWARD LEAR

The Little Creature

Twinkum, twankum, twirlum, twitch—
My great grandam—She was a Witch;
Mouse in Wainscot, Saint in niche—
My great grandam—She was a Witch;
Deadly nightshade flowers in a ditch—
My great grandam—She was a Witch;
Long though the shroud, it grows stitch by stitch—
My great grandam—She was a Witch;
Wean your weakling before you breech—
My great grandam—She was a Witch;
The fattest pig's but a double flitch—
My great grandam—She was a Witch;
Nightjars rattle, owls scritch—
My great grandam—She was a Witch.

  Pretty and small,
  A mere nothing at all,
  Pinned up sharp in the ghost of a shawl,
  She'd straddle her down to the kirkyard wall,
  And mutter and whisper and call,
  And call...

Red blood out and black blood in,
My Nannie says I'm a child of sin.
How did I choose me my witchcraft kin?

18

Know I as soon as dark's dreams begin
Snared is my heart in a nightmare's gin;
Never from terror I out may win;
So—dawn and dusk—I pine, peak, thin,
Scarcely beknowing t'other from which—
My great grandam—She was a Witch.

WALTER DE LA MARE

Witches' Charm

The owl is abroad, the bat, and the toad,
    And so is the cat-a-mountain,
The ant, and the mole sit both in a hole,
    And frog peeps out o' the fountain;
The dogs, they do bay, and the timbrels play,
    The spindle is now a-turning;
The moon it is red, and the stars are fled,
    But all the sky is a-burning:
The ditch is made, and our nails the spade,
With pictures full, of wax, and of wool;
Their livers I stick, with needles quick;
There lacks but the blood, to make up the flood.
    Quickly DAME, then, bring your part in,
    Spur, spur, upon little MARTIN,
    Merrily, merrily, make him sail,
    A worm in his mouth, and a thorn in's tail,
    Fire above, and fire below,
    With a whip i' your hand, to make him go.

    O, now she's come!
    Let all be dumb.   BEN JONSON

The Song of Quoodle

They haven't got no noses,
The fallen sons of Eve;
Even the smell of roses
Is not what they supposes;
But more than mind discloses
And more than men believe.

They haven't got no noses,
They cannot even tell
When door and darkness closes
The park a Jew encloses,
Where even the law of Moses
Will let you steal a smell.

The brilliant smell of water,
The brave smell of a stone,
The smell of dew and thunder,
The old bones buried under,
Are things in which they blunder
And err, if left alone.

The wind from winter forests,
The scent of scentless flowers,
The breath of brides' adorning,
The smell of snare and warning,
The smell of Sunday morning,
God gave to us for ours.

. . .

And Quoodle here discloses
All things that Quoodle can,
They haven't got no noses,
They haven't got no noses,
And goodness only knowses
The Noselessness of Man.

G. K. CHESTERTON

The Dong with a Luminous Nose

When awful darkness and silence reign
  Over the great Gromboolian plain,
    Through the long, long wintry nights;—
When the angry breakers roar,
As they beat on the rocky shore;—
    When Storm-clouds brood on the towering heights
Of the Hills of the Chankly Bore:—

Then, through the vast and gloomy dark,
There moves what seems a fiery spark,
   A lonely spark with silvery rays
   Piercing the coal-black night,—
   A meteor strange and bright:—
Hither and thither the vision strays,
   A single lurid light.

Slowly it wanders,—pauses,—creeps,—
Anon it sparkles,—flashes and leaps;
And ever as onward it gleaming goes
A light on the Bong-tree stems it throws.
And those who watch at that midnight hour
From Hall or Terrace, or lofty Tower,
Cry, as the wild light passes along,—
      'The Dong!—the Dong!
    The wandering Dong through the forest goes!
      The Dong! the Dong!
    The Dong with a luminous Nose!'

      Long years ago
    The Dong was happy and gay,
Till he fell in love with a Jumbly Girl
   Who came to those shores one day.
For the Jumblies came in a Sieve, they did,—
Landing at eve near the Zemmery Fidd
    Where the Oblong Oysters grow,
   And the rocks are smooth and gray.
And all the woods and the valleys rang
With the Chorus they daily and nightly sang,—
   'Far and few, far and few,
    Are the lands where the Jumblies live:
   Their heads are green, and their hands are blue,
    And they went to sea in a Sieve.'

Happily, happily passed those days!
    While the cheerful Jumblies staid;
   They danced in circlets all night long,
   To the plaintive pipe of the lively Dong,
    In moonlight, shine, or shade,

For day and night he was always there
By the side of the Jumbly Girl so fair,
With her sky-blue hands, and her sea-green hair.

Till the morning came of that hateful day
When the Jumblies sailed in their Sieve away,
And the Dong was left on the cruel shore
Gazing—gazing for evermore,—
Ever keeping his weary eyes on
That pea-green sail on the far horizon,—
Singing the Jumbly Chorus still
As he sat all day on the grassy hill,—
  'Far and few, far and few,
    Are the lands where the Jumblies live:
  Their heads are green, and their hands are blue,
    And they went to sea in a Sieve.'

But when the sun was low in the West,
    The Dong arose and said,—
  'What little sense I once possessed
    Has quite gone out of my head!'
And since that day he wanders still
By lake and forest, marsh and hill,
Singing—'O somewhere, in valley or plain
Might I find my Jumbly Girl again!
For ever I'll seek by lake and shore
Till I find my Jumbly Girl once more!'
        Playing a pipe with silvery squeaks,
        Since then his Jumbly Girl he seeks,
        And because by night he could not see,
        He gathered the bark of the Twangum Tree
          On the flowery plain that grows.
        And he wove him a wondrous Nose,—
        A Nose as strange as a Nose could be!
Of vast proportions and painted red,
And tied with cords to the back of his head.
        —In a hollow rounded space it ended
        With a luminous lamp within suspended,

All fenced about
With a bandage stout
  To prevent the wind from blowing it out;—
And with holes all round to send the light,
In gleaming rays on the dismal night.

And now each night, and all night long,
Over those plains still roams the Dong!
And above the wail of the Chimp and Snipe
You may hear the squeak of his plaintive pipe,
While ever he seeks, but seeks in vain,
To meet with his Jumbly Girl again;
Lonely and wild—all night he goes,—
The Dong with a luminous Nose!
And all who watch at the midnight hour,
From Hall or Terrace, or Lofty Tower,
Cry, as they trace the Meteor bright,
Moving along through the dreary night,—
         'This is the hour when forth he goes.
         The Dong with a luminous Nose!
         Yonder—over the plain he goes;
             He goes;
             He goes;
         The Dong with a luminous Nose!'

EDWARD LEAR

The Akond of Swat

Who, or why, or which, or *what*,   Is the Akond of SWAT?

Is he tall or short, or dark or fair?
Does he sit on a stool or a sofa or chair,   or SQUAT,
                                        The Akond of Swat?
Is he wise or foolish, young or old?
Does he drink his soup and his coffee cold,   or HOT,
                                        The Akond of Swat?
Does he sing or whistle, jabber or talk,
And when riding abroad does he gallop or walk,   or TROT,
                                        The Akond of Swat?

Does he wear a turban, a fez, or a hat?
Does he sleep on a mattress, a bed, or a mat,   or a COT,
       The Akond of Swat?

When he writes a copy in round-hand size,
Does he cross his T's and finish his I's   with a DOT,
       The Akond of Swat?

Can he write a letter concisely clear
Without a speck or a smudge or smear,   or BLOT,
       The Akond of Swat?

Do his people like him extremely well?
Or do they, whenever they can, rebel,   or PLOT,
       At the Akond of Swat?

If he catches them then, either old or young,
Does he have them chopped in pieces or hung,   or SHOT
       The Akond of Swat?

Do his people prig in the lanes or park?
Or even at times, when days are dark,   GAROTTE?
       O the Akond of Swat!

Does he study the wants of his own dominion?
Or doesn't he care for public opinion   a JOT,
       The Akond of Swat?

To amuse his mind do his people show him
Pictures, or anyone's last new poem,   or WHAT,
       For the Akond of Swat?

At night if he suddenly screams and wakes,
Do they bring him only a few small cakes,   or a LOT,
       For the Akond of Swat?

Does he live on turnips, tea, or tripe?
Does he like his shawl to be marked with a stripe,   or a DOT,
       The Akond of Swat?

Does he like to lie on his back in a boat
Like the lady who lived in that isle remote,   SHALLOTT,
       The Akond of Swat?

Is he quiet, or always making a fuss?
Is his steward a Swiss or a Swede or a Russ,   or a SCOT,
       The Akond of Swat?

Does he like to sit by the calm blue wave?
Or to sleep and snore in a dark green cave,   or a GROTT,
                The Akond of Swat?

Does he drink small beer from a silver jug?
Or a bowl? or a glass? or a cup? or a mug?   or a POT,
                The Akond of Swat?

Does he beat his wife with a gold-topped pipe,
When she lets the gooseberries grow too ripe,   or ROT,
                The Akond of Swat?

Does he wear a white tie when he dines with friends,
And tie it neat in a bow with ends,   or a KNOT,
                The Akond of Swat?

Does he like new cream, and hate mince-pies?
When he looks at the sun does he wink his eyes,   or NOT,
                The Akond of Swat?

Does he teach his subjects to roast and bake?
Does he sail about on an inland lake,   in a YACHT,
                The Akond of Swat?

Someone, or nobody, knows I wot
Who or which or why or what
                Is the Akond of Swat!

                EDWARD LEAR

Daniel

(A NEGRO'S INTERPRETATION OF THE BIBLE STORY)

Darius the Mede was a king and a wonder.
His eye was proud, and his voice was thunder.
He kept bad lions in a monstrous den.
He fed up the lions on Christian men.

Daniel was the chief hired man of the land.
He stirred up the music in the palace band.
He whitewashed the cellar. He shovelled in the coal.
And Daniel kept a-praying:—'Lord save my soul!'
Daniel kept a-praying:—'Lord save my soul!'
Daniel kept a-praying:—'Lord save my soul!'

Daniel was the butler, swagger and swell.
He ran up stairs. He answered the bell.
And *he* would let in whoever came a-calling—
Saints so holy, scamps so appalling.

Old man Ahab leaves his card.
Elisha and the bears are a-waiting in the yard.
Here comes Pharaoh and his snakes a-calling.
Here comes Cain and his wife a-calling.
Shadrach, Meshach and Abednego for tea.
Here comes Jonah, and the Whale,—
And the SEA!
And Daniel kept a-praying:—'Lord save my soul!'
Daniel kept a-praying:—'Lord save my soul!'
Daniel kept a-praying:—'Lord save my soul!'

His sweetheart and his mother were Christian and meek.
They washed and ironed for Darius every week.
One Thursday he met them at the door:
Paid them as usual, but acted sore.

He said:—'Your Daniel is a dead little pigeon.
He's a good hard worker, but he talks religion.'
And he showed them Daniel in the lions' cage,
Daniel standing quietly, the lions in a rage.
His good old mother cried:—'Lord save him!'
And Daniel's tender sweetheart cried:—'Lord save him!'

And she was a golden lily in the dew.
And she was as sweet as an apple on the tree,
And she was as fine as a melon in the corn-field,
Gliding and lovely as a ship on the sea,
Gliding and lovely as a ship on the sea.

And she prayed to the Lord:—
'Send Gabriel. Send Gabriel.'
King Darius said to the lions:—

'Bite Daniel. Bite Daniel.
Bite him. Bite him. Bite him!'

Thus roared the lions:—
'We want Daniel, Daniel, Daniel,
We want Daniel, Daniel, Daniel.'
Grrr—rrr—rrr...

And Daniel did not frown,
Daniel did not cry.
He kept on looking at the sky.
And the Lord said to Gabriel:—
'Go chain the lions down,
Go chain the lions down,
Go chain the lions down,
Go chain the lions down.'

And Gabriel chained the lions,
And Gabriel chained the lions,
And Gabriel chained the lions,
And Daniel got out of the den,
And Daniel got out of the den,
And Daniel got out of the den.

And Darius said:—'You're a Christian child.'
Darius said:—'You're a Christian child.'
Darius said:—'You're a Christian child.'
And gave him his job again,
And gave him his job again,
And gave him his job again.   VACHEL LINDSAY

The Congo

I. THEIR BASIC SAVAGERY

Fat black bucks in a wine-barrel room,
Barrel-house kings, with feet unstable,
Sagged and reeled and pounded on the table,
Pounded on the table,
Beat an empty barrel with the handle of a broom,
Hard as they were able,
Boom, boom, Boom,

A deep rolling
bass.

　　　　　bucks] men.

27

With a silk umbrella and the handle of a broom,
Boomlay, boomlay, boomlay, BOOM.
THEN I had religion, THEN I had a vision.
I could not turn from their revel in derision.

More deliberate.
Solemnly
chanted.

THEN I SAW THE CONGO, CREEPING THROUGH THE BLACK,
CUTTING THROUGH THE FOREST WITH A GOLDEN TRACK.
Then along that riverbank
A thousand miles
Tattooed cannibals danced in files;
Then I heard the boom of the blood-lust song

A rapidly piling
climax of speed
and racket.

And a thigh-bone beating on a tin-pan gong.
And 'BLOOD' screamed the whistles and the fifes of the
   warriors,
'BLOOD' screamed the skull-faced lean witch-doctors,
'Whirl ye the deadly voo-doo rattle,
Harry the uplands,
Steal all the cattle,
Rattle-rattle, rattle-rattle,
Bing.
Boomlay, boomlay, boomlay, BOOM,'

With a
philosophic
pause.

A roaring, epic, rag-time tune
From the mouth of the Congo
To the Mountains of the Moon.
Death is an Elephant,

Shrilly and with
a heavily
accented metre.

Torch-eyed and horrible,
Foam-flanked and terrible.
BOOM, steal the pygmies,
BOOM, kill the Arabs,
BOOM, kill the white men,
Hoo, Hoo, Hoo.

Like the wind in
the chimney.

Listen to the yell of Leopold's ghost
Burning in Hell for his hand-maimed host.
Hear how the demons chuckle and yell
Cutting his hands off, down in Hell.
Listen to the creepy proclamation,
Blown through the lairs of the forest-nation,
Blown past the white-ants' hill of clay,
Blown past the marsh where the butterflies play:—

'Be careful what you do,
Or Mumbo-Jumbo, God of the Congo,
And all of the other
Gods of the Congo,
Mumbo-Jumbo will hoo-doo you,
Mumbo-Jumbo will hoo-doo you,
Mumbo-Jumbo will hoo-doo you.'

*All the O
sounds very
golden.
Heavy accents
very heavy.
Light accents
very light. Last
line whispered.*

II. THEIR IRREPRESSIBLE HIGH SPIRITS

*Rather shrill
and high.*

Wild crap-shooters with a whoop and a call
Danced the juba in their gambling-hall
And laughed fit to kill, and shook the town,
And guyed the policemen and laughed them down
With a boomlay, boomlay, boomlay, BOOM.

*Read exactly as
in first section.*

THEN I SAW THE CONGO, CREEPING THROUGH THE BLACK,
CUTTING THROUGH THE FOREST WITH A GOLDEN TRACK.

*Lay emphasis
on the delicate
ideas.
Keep as light-
footed as
possible.*

A negro fairyland swung into view,
A minstrel river
Where dreams come true.
The ebony palace soared on high
Through the blossoming trees to the evening sky.
The inlaid porches and casements shone
With gold and ivory and elephant-bone.
And the black crowd laughed till their sides were sore
At the baboon butler in the agate door,
And the well-known tunes of the parrot band
That trilled on the bushes of that magic land.

With pomposity.

A troupe of skull-faced witch-men came
Through the agate doorway in suits of flame,
Yea, long-tailed coats with a gold-leaf crust ·
And hats that were covered with diamond-dust.
And the crowd in the court gave a whoop and a call
And danced the juba from wall to wall.

*With a great
deliberation and
ghostliness.*

But the witch-men suddenly stilled the throng
With a stern cold glare, and a stern old song:—
'Mumbo-Jumbo will hoo-doo you'...

29

<table>
<tr>
<td>With over-
whelming
assurance, good
cheer, and
pomp.</td>
<td>Just then from the doorway, as fat as shotes,
Came the cake-walk princes in their long red coats,
Canes with a brilliant lacquer shine,
And tall silk hats that were red as wine.</td>
</tr>
<tr>
<td>With growing
speed and
sharply marked
dance-rhythm.</td>
<td>And they pranced with their butterfly partners there,
Coal-black maidens with pearls in their hair,
Knee-skirts trimmed with the jassamine sweet,
And bells on their ankles and little black feet.
And the couples railed at the chant and the frown
Of the witch-men lean, and laughed them down.
(O rare was the revel, and well worth while
That made those glowering witch-men smile.)</td>
</tr>
</table>

The cake-walk royalty then began
To walk for a cake that was tall as a man
To the tune of 'Boomlay, boomlay, BOOM'.

<table>
<tr>
<td>With a touch of
negro dialect,
and as rapidly as
possible toward
the end.</td>
<td>While the witch-men laughed, with a sinister air,
And sang with the scalawags prancing there:—
'Walk with care, walk with care,
Or Mumbo-Jumbo, God of the Congo,
And all of the other
Gods of the Congo,
Mumbo-Jumbo will hoo-doo you.
Beware, beware, walk with care,
Boomlay, boomlay, boomlay, boom.
Boomlay, boomlay, boomlay, boom,
Boomlay, boomlay, boomlay, boom,
Boomlay, boomlay, boomlay,
BOOM.'</td>
</tr>
<tr>
<td>Slow philo-
sophic calm.</td>
<td>Oh rare was the revel, and well worth while
That made those glowering witch-men smile.</td>
</tr>
</table>

III. THE HOPE OF THEIR RELIGION

<table>
<tr>
<td>Heavy bass.
With a literal
imitation of
camp-meeting
racket, and
trance.</td>
<td>A good old negro in the slums of the town
Preached at a sister for her velvet gown.
Howled at a brother for his low-down ways,
His prowling, guzzling, sneak-thief days.</td>
</tr>
</table>

shotes] porkers.

30

Beat on the Bible till he wore it out
Starting the jubilee revival shout.
And some had visions, as they stood on chairs,
And sang of Jacob, and the golden stairs,
And they all repented, a thousand strong
From their stupor and savagery and sin and wrong
And slammed with their hymn books till they shook the
room
With 'glory, glory, glory,'
And 'Boom, boom, BOOM.'

Exactly as in the first section. Begin with terror and power, end with joy.

THEN I SAW THE CONGO, CREEPING THROUGH THE BLACK
CUTTING THROUGH THE JUNGLE WITH A GOLDEN TRACK.
And the gray sky opened like a new-rent veil
And showed the Apostles with their coats of mail.
In bright white steel they were seated round
And their fire-eyes watched where the Congo wound.
And the twelve Apostles, from their thrones on high
Thrilled all the forest with their heavenly cry:—

Sung to the tune of 'Hark, ten thousand harps and voices.'

'Mumbo-Jumbo will die in the jungle;
Never again will he hoo-doo you,
Never again will he hoo-doo you.'

With growing deliberation and joy.

Then along that river, a thousand miles
The vine-snared trees fell down in files.
Pioneer angels cleared the way
For a Congo paradise, for babes at play,
For sacred capitals, for temples clean.
Gone were the skull-faced witch-men lean.

In a rather high key—as delicately as possible.

There, where the wild ghost-gods had wailed
A million boats of the angels sailed
With oars of silver, and prows of blue
And silken pennants that the sun shone through
'Twas a land transfigured, 'twas a new creation.
Oh, a singing wind swept the negro nation
And on through the backwoods clearing flew:—

To the tune of 'Hark, ten thousand harps and voices.'

'Mumbo-Jumbo is dead in the jungle.
Never again will he hoo-doo you.
Never again will he hoo-doo you.'

31

Redeemed were the forests, the beasts and the men,
And only the vulture dared again
By the far, lone Mountains of the Moon
To cry, in the silence, the Congo tune:—
Dying down into a penetrating, terrified whisper. 'Mumbo-Jumbo will hoo-doo you,
Mumbo-Jumbo will hoo-doo you,
Mumbo...Jumbo...will...hoo-doo...you.'

VACHEL LINDSAY

PICTURES IN WORDS

We often find that some words are much more effective than others in describing the things we see. When words are carefully chosen the picture in words may be so vivid or so unusual as to give us an immediate feeling of pleasure.

This is how a Chinese coolie described in Pidgin English a three-masted, screw-driven steamer with two funnels:

Three piecee bamboo, two piecee puff-puff, walk-along-inside, no can see.

You will easily guess that the 'walk-along-inside' is the engine which makes the ship move and, being inside, cannot be seen.

In the same poetic way 'Don't you know the bald-headed white man?' becomes 'You no savvy that fellow white man coconut belong him no grass.' A piano is described as 'a big fellow box, you fight him he shout out.'

This picturesque description:

> Four stiff-standers
> Four dilly danders
> Two lookers, two crookers
> And a wig-wag

is found in so many different languages that it has been called a 'world-riddle'. It is a picture of a cow, and can be traced, it is said, for thousands of years through the traditional expression of many different nations.

It is a kind of poetry. When the native servant says, 'What for lamp you make him dead?' meaning 'Why have you put out the light?', he is very close to the poet who writes:

> When the lamp is shattered
> The light in the dust lies dead.

Very often a poet will arrest and hold our attention by his choice of epithets, the describing words, and verbs, which enliven the scene:

> Little trotty wagtail, you *nimble* all about
> And in the *dimpling* water-pudge you *waddle* in and out.

The epithet compresses the meaning, often packing a whole sentence into one word:

> The *wrinkled* sea beneath him crawls.

Look at this vivid picture in two lines:

> And birds sit *brooding* in the snow,
> And Marian's nose looks *red* and *raw*.

You will see that poetry uses words in a vivid and at the same time precise way, creating pictures that live in your mind.

Three Young Rats

Three young rats with black felt hats,
Three young ducks with white straw flats,
Three young dogs with curling tails,
Three young cats with demi-veils,
Went out to walk with two young pigs
In satin vests and sorrel wigs;
But suddenly it chanced to rain,
And so they all went home again.

34

Little Trotty Wagtail

Little trotty wagtail, he went in the rain,
And tittering, tottering sideways he ne'er got straight again.
He stooped to get a worm, and looked up to get a fly,
And then he flew away ere his feathers they were dry.

Little trotty wagtail, he waddled in the mud,
And left his little footmarks, trample where he would.
He waddled in the water-pudge, and waggle went his tail,
And chirrup up his wings to dry upon the garden rail.

Little trotty wagtail, you nimble all about,
And in the dimpling water-pudge you waddle in and out;
Your home is nigh at hand, and in the warm pig-sty,
So, little Master Wagtail, I'll bid you a good-bye.

JOHN CLARE

Blackbird

He comes on chosen evenings,
My blackbird bountiful, and sings
Over the gardens of the town
Just at the hour the sun goes down.
His flight across the chimneys thick,
By some divine arithmetic,
Comes to his customary stack
And couches there his plumage black,
And there he lifts his yellow bill,
Kindled against the sunset, till
These suburbs are like Dymock woods
Where music has her solitudes,
And while he mocks the winter's wrong,
Rapt on his pinnacle of song,
Figured above our garden plots
Those are celestial chimney-pots.

JOHN DRINKWATER

Dymock: a village in Gloucestershire, a few miles south of Ledbury.

The Eagle

He clasps the crag with crooked hands;
Close to the sun in lonely lands,
Ringed with the azure world he stands.

The wrinkled sea beneath him crawls;
He watches from his mountain-walls,
And like a thunderbolt he falls.

LORD TENNYSON

The Eagle

He hangs between his wings outspread
Level and still
And bends a narrow golden head,
Scanning the ground to kill,

Though as he sails and smoothly swings
Round the hill-side,
He looks as though from his own wings
He hung down crucified.

ANDREW YOUNG

The Hawk

The hawk slipt out of the pine, and rose in the sunlit air:
Steady and still he poised; his shadow slept on the grass:
And the bird's song sickened and sank: she cowered with furtive
        stare,
Dumb, till the quivering dimness should flicker and shift and pass.
Suddenly down he dropped: she heard the hiss of his wing,
Fled with a scream of terror: oh, would she had dared to rest!
For the hawk at eve was full, and there was no bird to sing,
And over the heather drifted the down from a bleeding breast.

A. C. BENSON

36

Silver

Slowly, silently, now the moon
Walks the night in her silver shoon;
This way, and that, she peers, and sees
Silver fruit upon silver trees;
One by one the casements catch
Her beams beneath the silvery thatch;
Couched in his kennel, like a log,
With paws of silver sleeps the dog;
From their shadowy cote the white breasts peep
Of doves in a silver-feathered sleep;
A harvest mouse goes scampering by,
With silver claws, and silver eye;
And moveless fish in the water gleam,
By silver reeds in a silver stream.

WALTER DE LA MARE

Moonlit Apples

At the top of the house the apples are laid in rows,
And the skylight lets the moonlight in, and those
Apples are deep-sea apples of green. There goes
  A cloud on the moon in the autumn night.

A mouse in the wainscot scratches, and scratches, and then
There is no sound at the top of the house of men
Or mice; and the cloud is blown, and the moon again
  Dapples the apples with deep-sea light.

They are lying in rows there, under the gloomy beams;
On the sagging floor; they gather the silver streams
Out of the moon, those moonlit apples of dreams,
  And quiet is the steep stair under.

In the corridors under there is nothing but sleep.
And stiller than ever on orchard boughs they keep
Tryst with the moon, and deep is the silence, deep
  On moon-washed apples of wonder.

JOHN DRINKWATER

37

The Pool in the Rock

In this water, clear as air,
Lurks a lobster in its lair.
Rock-bound weed sways out and in,
Coral-red, and bottle-green.
Wondrous pale anemones
Stir like flowers in a breeze:
Fluted scallop, whelk in shell,
And the prowling mackerel.
Winged with snow the sea-mews ride
The brine-keen wind; and far and wide
Sounds on the hollow thunder of the tide.

WALTER DE LA MARE

Nicholas Nye

Thistle and darnel and dock grew there,
    And a bush, in the corner, of may,
On the orchard wall I used to sprawl
    In the blazing heat of the day;
Half asleep and half awake,
    While the birds went twittering by,
And nobody there my love to share
    But Nicholas Nye.

Nicholas Nye was lean and grey,
    Lame of a leg and old,
More than a score of donkey's years
    He had seen since he was foaled;
He munched the thistles, purple and spiked,
    Would sometimes stoop and sigh,
And turn his head, as if he said,
    'Poor Nicholas Nye!'

Alone with his shadow he'd drowse in the meadow,
    Lazily swinging his tail,
At break of day he used to bray,—
    Not much too hearty and hale;

But a wonderful gumption was under his skin,
  And a clear calm light in his eye,
And once in a while: he'd smile...
    Would Nicholas Nye.

Seem to be smiling at me, he would,
  From his bush in the corner, of may,—
Bony and ownerless, widowed and worn,
  Knobble-kneed, lonely and grey;
And over the grass would seem to pass
  'Neath the deep dark blue of the sky,
Something much better than words between me
    And Nicholas Nye.

But dusk would come in the apple boughs,
  The green of the glow-worm shine,
The birds in nest would crouch to rest,
  And home I'd trudge to mine;
And there, in the moonlight, dark with dew,
  Asking not wherefore nor why,
Would brood like a ghost, and as still as a post,
    Old Nicholas Nye.   WALTER DE LA MARE

The Poor Man's Pig

Already fallen plum-bloom stars the green,
  And apple-boughs as knarred as old toads' backs
Wear their small roses ere a rose is seen;
  The building thrush watches old Job who stacks
The fresh-peeled osiers on the sunny fence,
  The pent sow grunts to hear him stumping by,
And tries to push the bolt and scamper thence,
  But her ringed snout still keeps her to the sty.
Then out he lets her run; away she snorts
  In bundling gallop for the cottage door,
With hungry hubbub begging crusts and orts,
  Then like the whirlwind bumping round once more;
Nuzzling the dog, making the pullets run,
And sulky as a child when her play's done.
                    EDMUND BLUNDEN

39

Milk for the Cat

When the tea is brought at five o'clock,
And all the neat curtains are drawn with care,
The little black cat with bright green eyes
Is suddenly purring there.

At first she pretends, having nothing to do,
She has come in merely to blink by the grate,
But, though tea may be late or the milk may be sour,
She is never late.

And presently her agate eyes
Take a soft large milky haze,
And her independent casual glance
Becomes a stiff, hard gaze.

Then she stamps her claws or lifts her ears,
Or twists her tail and begins to stir,
Till suddenly all her lithe body becomes
One breathing, trembling purr.

The children eat and wriggle and laugh;
The two old ladies stroke their silk:
But the cat is grown small and thin with desire,
Transformed to a creeping lust for milk:

The white saucer like some full moon descends
At last from the clouds of the table above;
She sighs and dreams and thrills and glows,
Transfigured with love.

She nestles over the shining rim,
Buries her chin in the creamy sea;
Her tail hangs loose; each drowsy paw
Is doubled under each bending knee.

A long dim ecstasy holds her life;
Her world is an infinite shapeless white,
Till her tongue has curled the last half drop,
Then she sinks back into the night,

Draws and dips her body to heap
Her sleepy nerves in the great arm-chair,
Lies defeated and buried deep
Three or four hours unconscious there.

HAROLD MONRO

Ducks

I

From troubles of the world
I turn to ducks,
Beautiful comical things,
Sleeping or curled
Their heads beneath white wings
By water cool,
Or finding curious things
To eat in various mucks
Beneath the pool,
Tails uppermost, or waddling
Sailor-like on the shores
Of ponds, or paddling
—Left! right!—with fanlike feet
Which are for steady oars
When they (white galleys) float
Each bird a boat
Rippling at will the sweet
Wide waterway...
When night is fallen *you* creep
Upstairs, but drakes and dillies
Nest with pale water-stars,
Moonbeams and shadow bars,
And water-lilies:
Fearful too much to sleep
Since they've no locks
To click against the teeth
Of weasel and fox.
And warm beneath
Are eggs of cloudy green
Whence hungry rats and lean

Would stealthily suck
New life, but for the mien,
The bold ferocious mien
Of the mother-duck.

II

Yes, ducks are valiant things
On nests of twigs and straws,
And ducks are soothy things
And lovely on the lake
When that the sunlight draws
Thereon their pictures dim
In colours cool.
And when beneath the pool
They dabble, and when they swim
And make their rippling rings,
O ducks are beautiful things!

But ducks are comical things—
As comical as you.
Quack!
They waddle round, they do.
They eat all sorts of things,
And then they quack.
By barn and stable and stack
They wander at their will,
But if you go too near
They look at you through black
Small topaz-tinted eyes
And wish you ill.
Triangular and clear
They leave their curious track
In mud at the water's edge,
And there amid the sedge
And slime they gobble and peer,
Saying 'Quack! Quack!'

III

When God had finished the stars and whirl of coloured suns
He turned His mind from big things to fashion little ones,
Beautiful tiny things (like daisies) He made, and then
He made the comical ones in case the minds of men
      Should stiffen and become
      Dull, humourless and glum;
And so forgetful of their Maker be
As to take even themselves—*quite seriously*.
Caterpillars and cats are lively and excellent puns:
All God's jokes are good—even the practical ones!
And as for the duck, I think God must have smiled a bit
Seeing those bright eyes blink on the day He fashioned it.
And He's probably laughing still at the sound that came out
    of its bill!   **F. W. HARVEY**

Tall Nettles

Tall nettles cover up, as they have done
These many springs, the rusty harrow, the plough
Long worn out, and the roller made of stone:
Only the elm butt tops the nettles now.

This corner of the farmyard I like most:
As well as any bloom upon a flower
I like the dust on the nettles, never lost
Except to prove the sweetness of a shower.
               EDWARD THOMAS

Weathers

This is the weather the cuckoo likes,
    And do so I;
When showers betumble the chestnut spikes,
    And nestlings fly;
And the little brown nightingale bills his best,
And they sit outside at 'The Travellers' Rest',

And maids come forth sprig-muslin drest,
And citizens dream of the south and west,
    And so do I.

This is the weather the shepherd shuns,
        And so do I;
When beeches drip in browns and duns,
        And thresh, and ply;
And hill-hid tides throb, throe on throe,
And meadow rivulets overflow,
And drops on gate-bars hang in a row,
And rooks in families homeward go,
        And so do I.   THOMAS HARDY

Winter

When icicles hang by the wall,
    And Dick the shepherd blows his nail,
And Tom bears logs into the hall,
    And milk comes frozen home in pail,
When blood is nipp'd and ways be foul,
Then nightly sings the staring owl,
                    To-whit!
To-who!—a merry note,
While greasy Joan doth keel the pot.

When all aloud the wind doth blow,
    And coughing drowns the parson's saw,
And birds sit brooding in the snow,
    And Marian's nose looks red and raw,
When roasted crabs hiss in the bowl,
Then nightly sings the staring owl,
                    To-whit!
To-who!—a merry note,
While greasy Joan doth keel the pot.
                WILLIAM SHAKESPEARE

crabs] apples.

44

Miss Thompson Goes Shopping

A little farther down the way
Stands Miles's fish-shop, whence is shed
So strong a smell of fishes dead
That people of a subtler sense
Hold their breath and hurry thence.
Miss Thompson hovers there and gazes:
Her housewife's knowing eye appraises
Salt and fresh, severely cons
Kippers bright as tarnished bronze:
Great cods disposed upon the sill,
Chilly and wet, with gaping gill,
Flat head, glazed eye, and mute, uncouth,
Shapeless, wan, old-woman's mouth.
Next a row of soles and plaice
With querulous and twisted face,
And red-eyed bloaters, golden-grey;
Smoked haddocks ranked in neat array;
A group of smelts that take the light
Like slips of rainbow, pearly bright;
Silver trout with rosy spots,
And coral shrimps with keen black dots
For eyes, and hard and jointed sheath
And crisp tails curving underneath.
But there upon the sanded floor,
More wonderful in all that store
Than anything on slab or shelf,
Stood Miles, the fishmonger, himself.
Four-square he stood and filled the place.
His huge hands and his jolly face
Were red. He had a mouth to quaff
Pint after pint; a sounding laugh,
But wheezy at the end, and oft
His eyes bulged outwards and he coughed.
Aproned he stood from chin to toe,
The apron's vertical long flow
Warped grandly outwards to display

45

His hale round belly hung midway,
Whose apex was securely bound
With apron-strings wrapped round and round.
Outside, Miss Thompson, small and staid,
Felt, as she always felt, afraid
Of this huge man who laughed so loud
And drew the notice of the crowd.
Awhile she paused in timid thought,
Then promptly hurried in and bought
'Two kippers, please. Yes, lovely weather,'
'Two kippers? Sixpence altogether.'
And in the basket laid the pair
Wrapped face to face in newspaper.

MARTIN ARMSTRONG

The Great Lover

These I have loved:
        White plates and cups, clean-gleaming,
Ringed with blue lines; and feathery, faery dust;
Wet roofs, beneath the lamp-light; the strong crust
Of friendly bread; and many-tasting food;
Rainbows; and the blue bitter smoke of wood;
And radiant raindrops couching in cool flowers;
And flowers themselves, that sway through sunny hours,
Dreaming of moths that drink them under the moon;
Then, the cool kindliness of sheets, that soon
Smooth away trouble; and the rough male kiss
Of blankets; grainy wood; live hair that is
Shining and free; blue-massing clouds; the keen
Unpassioned beauty of a great machine;
The benison of hot water; furs to touch;
The good smell of old clothes; and other such—
The comfortable smell of friendly fingers,
Hair's fragrance, and the musty reek that lingers
About dead leaves and last year's ferns...
                        Dear names,
And thousand others throng to me! Royal flames;

Sweet water's dimpling laugh from tap or spring;
Holes in the ground; and voices that do sing:
Voices in laughter, too; and body's pain,
Soon turned to peace; and the deep-panting train;
Firm sands; the little dulling edge of foam
That browns and dwindles as the wave goes home;
And washen stones, gay for an hour; the cold
Graveness of iron; moist black earthen mould;
Sleep; and high places; footprints in the dew;
And oaks; and brown horse-chestnuts, glossy-new;
And new-peeled sticks; and shining pools on grass;—
All these have been my loves.   RUPERT BROOKE

SECTION 3

TALES AND MINSTRELSY

From our very early days we love to hear stories, and you will recall how much nursery rhymes appealed to you at one time, particularly those that told a tale. You may remember the one beginning:

> A frog he would a-wooing go,

which tells the story of the adventurous Anthony Rowley, who wore an opera hat, made friends with a rat and a mouse and proceeded to merry-making at Mrs Mouse's hall.

> With a rowley, powley, gammon and spinach
> Heigh ho! says Anthony Rowley.

The party broke up on the unexpected arrival of a cat and her kittens, and, when hurriedly crossing a brook on his way home, poor Rowley was gobbled up by a lily-white duck.

These rhymes are full of invention, with lively incidents, and memorable characters such as Miss Muffet, Mother Hubbard, Little Jack Horner; and have given delight to children for hundreds of years.

It is interesting to know that the great majority of nursery rhymes were not in the first place composed for children. They have many different origins. The earliest are echoes of ancient custom and ritual, and memories of proverbial sayings; but far more frequently they are fragments of old ballads or of folk-songs.

Though these folk-songs and ballads belong to an older tradition than nursery rhymes they have something in common, and have come down to us in much the same way.

As the name implies, folk-songs were the songs of the people, and, like nursery rhymes, were of unknown authorship. Some were work-songs, such as sea shanties, helping men to keep together while doing some rhythmical job. Others told a simple story and were said or sung by a minstrel where people gathered together. When the story ended we can imagine the audience saying 'tell it again, and tell it just the same', rejecting any variation from the original recital, just as children do when they hear a nursery rhyme for the first time. This would fix the folk-song in people's memories, and it would be passed from one generation to the next by word of mouth, for ballads and folk-songs and early tales were not written down for many, many years.

The themes of such traditional tales are extremely varied. Sometimes the story is about some simple incident connected with an animal, as in the folk-song:

The Fox jumped up on a moonlight night

with the Fox, old Gammer Hipple-Hopple and the Farmer playing out the action. Sometimes it is based on a real story, perhaps some gossip or local scandal known in a particular district. Such is *The Frolicsome Duke*, which tells a story about a real person, Philip the Good, Duke of Burgundy.

Occasionally a person would become popular because of his adventurous life, and a series of stories would grow up round his name, until, finally, he would become a legend. Robin Hood is such a figure, and there are many tales in verse about him, a part of the minstrelsy of early days.

The Pied Piper and *The Jackdaw of Rheims*, written much closer to our own time, recapture the zest and liveliness of the early tales with a wonderful cascade of words as enjoyable as the story they tell.

Green Broom

There was an old man and he lived in the West,
And his trade was the cutting of broom, green broom;
He had but one son, whose name it was John,
Who'd lie in his bed till noon, till noon,
Who'd lie in his bed till noon.

The old man arose and to his son goes,
And swore he would fire the room, the room,
If John wouldna rise and sharp up his knives
And go to the wood to cut broom, green broom,
And go to the wood to cut broom.

Then John he arose and put on his clothes;
He banned and he swore and did fume, did fume,
To think that he should, with his breeding so good,
Be doomed all his life to cut broom, green broom,
Be doomed all his life to cut broom.

So John he passed on to the Greenwood alone,
Till he came to a castle of gloom, grey gloom;
He rapped at the gate where'er he could beat,
Crying 'Maids, will you buy my green broom, green broom?'
Crying 'Maids, will you buy my green broom?'

A lady on high did him then espy,
And marvelling much at his bloom, bright bloom,
She called on her maid to use all her speed
And bring up the youth with his broom, green broom,
And bring up the youth with his broom.

John climbed the dark stair without dread or fear,
Till he came to this fair lady's room, fine room;
With courtesy kind he pleased so her mind,
She asked him there for her groom, bridegroom,
She asked him there for her groom.

Now all ye broom-cutters that live in the West,
Pray call at the castle of gloom, grey gloom;
There's both meat and drink, lads, and what do you think?—
No trade like the cutting o' broom, green broom,
No trade like the cutting o' broom.

The Wraggle-taggle Gipsies

Three gipsies came to the castle gate,
　　And downstairs ran this a-lady, O!
One sang high, and another sang low,
　　And the other sang, Bonny, bonny, Biscay, O!

Then she pulled off her silk-finished gown
　　And put on hose of leather, O!
The ragged, ragged rags about our door—
　　She's gone with the wraggle-taggle gipsies, O!

It was late last night, when my lord came home,
　　Inquiring for his a-lady, O!
The servants said, on every hand:
　　'She's gone with the wraggle-taggle gipsies, O!'

'O saddle to me my milk-white steed,
　　Go and fetch me my pony, O!
That I may ride and seek my bride,
　　Who is gone with the wraggle-taggle gipsies, O!'

O he rode high and he rode low,
　　He rode through woods and copses, O!
Until he came to an open field,
　　And there he espied his a-lady, O!

'What makes you leave your house and land?
　　What makes you leave your money, O?
What makes you leave your new-wedded lord;
　　To go with the wraggle-taggle gipsies, O?'

'What care I for my house and my land?
  What care I for my money, O?
What care I for my new-wedded lord?
  I'm off with the wraggle-taggle gipsies, O!'

'Last night you slept on a goose-feather bed,
  With the sheet turned down so bravely, O!
And to-night you'll sleep in a cold open field,
  Along with the wraggle-taggle gipsies, O!'

'What care I for a goose-feather bed,
  With the sheet turned down so bravely, O?
For to-night I shall sleep in a cold open field,
  Along with the wraggle-taggle gipsies, O!'

The Fox jumped up on a Moonlight Night

The fox jumped up on a moonlight night,
The stars they were shining and all things bright;
'Oh, ho!' said the fox, 'it's a very fine night
  For me to go over the down, O.'

The fox soon came to a farmer's yard,
Where the ducks and the geese were sore afeared;
'The best of you all shall grease my beard
  When I trot home to my den, O.'

Old Gammer Hipple-Hopple hopped out of bed,
She opened the casement and popped out her head;
'Oh, husband! oh, husband! the grey goose is dead,
  And the fox is gone through the town, O.'

The fox and his wife, without any strife,
They cut up the goose without fork and knife,
And said 'twas the best they had eat in their life,
  And the young ones picked the bones, O.

A Farmer he lived in the West Country

A Farmer he lived in the West country,
    Bow down! Bow down!
A Farmer he lived in the West country
And he had daughters one, two and three,
Singing 'I will be true unto my love
If my love will be true unto me.'

One day they walked by the river's brim,
    Bow down! Bow down!
One day they walked by the river's brim
When the eldest pushed the youngest in,
Singing 'I will be true unto my love
If my love will be true unto me.'

'O sister, O sister, pray lend me your hand,'
    Bow down! Bow down!
'O sister, O sister, pray lend me your hand
And I'll give you both house and land,'
Singing 'I will be true unto my love
If my love will be true unto me.'

'I'll neither lend you hand nor glove,'
    Bow down! Bow down!
'I'll neither lend you hand nor glove
Unless you'll promise me your true love,'
Singing 'I will be true unto my love
If my love will be true unto me.'

So down the river the maiden swam,
    Bow down! Bow down!
So down the river the maiden swam
Until she came to the miller's dam,
Singing 'I will be true unto my love
If my love will be true unto me.'

The miller's daughter stood at the door,
    Bow down! Bow down!
The miller's daughter stood at the door

Blooming like a gilliflower,
Singing 'I will be true unto my love
If my love will be true unto me.'

'O father, O father, here swims a swan,'
    Bow down! Bow down!
'O father, O father, here swims a swan
Very much like a gentlewoman,'
Singing 'I will be true unto my love
If my love will be true unto me.'

The miller he took his rod and hook,
    Bow down! Bow down!
The miller he took his rod and hook.
And he fished the fair maiden out of the brook,
Singing 'I will be true unto my love
If my love will be true unto me.'

The Frolicsome Duke

Now as fame does report a young duke keeps a court,
One that pleases his fancy with frolicsome sport:
But amongst all the rest, here is one I protest,
Which will make you to smile when you hear the true jest:
A poor tinker he found, lying drunk on the ground,
As secure in a sleep as if laid in a swound.

The duke said to his men, William, Richard and Ben,
'Take him home to my palace, we'll sport with him then.'
O'er a horse he was laid, and with care soon convey'd
To the palace, altho' he was poorly array'd:
Then they stript off his clothes, both his shirt, shoes and hose,
And they put him to bed for to take his repose.

Having pull'd off his shirt, which was all over dirt,
They did give him clean holland, this was no great hurt:
On a bed of soft down, like a lord of renown,
They did lay him to sleep the drink out of his crown.
In the morning when day, then admiring he lay,
For to see the rich chamber both gaudy and gay.

Now he lay something late, in his rich bed of state,
Till at last knights and squires they on him did wait;
And the chamberlain bare, then did likewise declare,
He desired to know what apparel he'd wear:
The poor tinker amaz'd, on the gentleman gaz'd,
And admired how he to this honour was rais'd.

Tho' he seem'd something mute, yet he chose a rich suit,
Which he straitways put on without longer dispute:
With a star on his side, which the tinker oft ey'd,
And it seem'd for to swell him no little with pride;
For he said to himself, 'Where is Joan my sweet wife?
Sure she never did see me so fine in her life.'

From a convenient place, the right duke his good grace
Did observe his behaviour in every case.
To a garden of state, on the tinker they wait,
Trumpets sounding before him: thought he, this is great:
Where an hour or two, pleasant walks he did view,
With commanders and squires in scarlet and blue.

A fine dinner was drest, both for him and his guests,
He was plac'd at the table above all the rest,
In a rich chair or bed, lin'd with fine crimson red,
With a rich golden canopy over his head:
As he sat at his meat, the music play'd sweet,
With the choicest of singing his joys to complete.

While the tinker did dine, he had plenty of wine,
Rich canary with sherry and tent superfine.
Like a right honest soul, faith, he took off his bowl,
Till at last he began for to tumble and roll
From his chair to the floor, where he sleeping did snore,
Being seven times drunker than ever before.

Then the duke did ordain, they should strip him amain,
And restore him his old leather garments again:

tent] deep-red wine.

55

'Twas a point next the worst, yet perform it they must,
And they carried him strait, where they found him at first;
Then he slept all the night, as indeed well he might;
But when he did waken, his joys took their flight.

For his glory to him so pleasant did seem,
That he thought it to be but a mere golden dream;
Till at length he was brought to the duke, where he sought
For a pardon, as fearing he had set him at nought;
But his highness he said, 'Thou'rt a jolly bold blade,
Such a frolic before I think never was played.'

Then his highness bespoke him a new suit and cloak,
Which he gave for the sake of this frolicsome joke;
Nay, and five-hundred pound, with ten acres of ground,
'Thou shalt never,' said he, 'range the countries around,
Crying old brass to mend, for I'll be thy good friend,
Nay, and Joan thy sweet wife shall my duchess attend.'

Then the tinker replied, 'What! must Joan my sweet bride
Be a lady in chariots of pleasure to ride?
Must we have gold and land ev'ry day at command?
Then I shall be a squire I well understand:
Well I thank your good grace, and your love I embrace,
I was never before in so happy a case.'

Meet-on-the-Road

'Now, pray, where are you going?' said Meet-on-the-Road.
'To school, sir, to school, sir,' said Child-as-it-Stood.

'What have you in your basket, child?' said Meet-on-the-Road.
'My dinner, sir, my dinner, sir,' said Child-as-it-Stood.

'What have you for dinner, child?' said Meet-on-the-Road.
'Some pudding, sir, some pudding, sir,' said Child-as-it-Stood.

'Oh, then I pray, give me a share,' said Meet-on-the-Road.
'I've little enough for myself, sir,' said Child-as-it-Stood.

'What have you got that cloak on for?' said Meet-on-the-Road.
'To keep the wind and cold from me,' said Child-as-it-Stood.

'I wish the wind would blow through you,' said Meet-on-the-Road.
'Oh, what a wish! What a wish!' said Child-as-it-Stood.

'Pray what are those bells ringing for?' said Meet-on-the-Road.
'To ring bad spirits home again,' said Child-as-it-Stood.

'Oh, then I must be going, child!' said Meet-on-the-Road.
'So fare you well, so fare you well,' said Child-as-it-Stood.

The Mermaid

One Friday morn when we set sail,
    Not very far from land,
We there did espy a fair pretty maid
    With a comb and a glass in her hand, her hand, her hand,
    With a comb and a glass in her hand.
      While the raging seas did roar,
        And the stormy winds did blow,
      While we jolly sailor-boys were up into the top,
        And the land-lubbers lying down below, below, below,
        And the land-lubbers lying down below.

Then up starts the captain of our gallant ship,
    And a brave young man was he:
'I've a wife and a child in fair Bristol town,
    But a widow I fear she will be.'
      And the raging seas did roar,
        And the stormy winds did blow.

Then up starts the mate of our gallant ship,
    And a bold young man was he:
'Oh! I have a wife in fair Portsmouth town,
    But a widow I fear she will be.'
      And the raging seas did roar,
        And the stormy winds did blow.

Then up starts the cook of our gallant ship,
  And a gruff old soul was he:
'Oh! I have a wife in fair Plymouth town,
  But a widow I fear she will be.'
    And the raging seas did roar,
    And the stormy winds did blow.

And then up spoke the little cabin-boy,
  And a pretty little boy was he;
'Oh! I am more grieved for my daddy
  Than you for your wives all three.'
    And the raging seas did roar,
    And the stormy winds did blow.

Then three times round went our gallant ship,
  And three times round went she;
And three times round went our gallant ship,
  And she sank to the bottom of the sea....

    And the raging seas did roar,
    And the stormy winds did blow,
    While we jolly sailor-boys were up into the top,
    And the land-lubbers lying down below, below, below,
    And the land-lubbers lying down below.

Saddle to Rags

This story I'm going to sing,
  I hope it will give you content,
Concerning a silly old man
  That was going to pay his rent.
    With a till da dill, till a dill, dill,
    Till a dill, dill a dill, dee.

As he was a-riding along,
  Along all on the highway,
A gentleman-thief overtook him,
  And thus unto him he did say:

'O! well overtaken, old man,
  O! well overtaken,' said he:
'Thank you kindly, sir,' says the old man,
  'If you be for my company.'

'How far are you going this way?'
  It made the old man to smile;
'To tell you the truth, kind sir,
  I'm just a-going twa mile.

'I am but a silly old man,
  Who farms a piece of ground;
My half-year rent, kind sir,
  Just comes to forty pound.

'But my landlord's not been at hame,
  I've not seen him twelve month or more;
It makes my rent to be large,
  I've just to pay him fourscore.'

'You should not have told anybody,
  For thieves they are ganging many;
If they were to light upon you
  They would rob you of every penny.'

'O! never mind,' says the old man,
  'Thieves I fear on no side;
My money is safe in my bags,
  In the saddle on which I ride.'

As they were a-riding along,
  And riding a-down a ghyll,
The thief pulled out a pistol,
  And bade the old man stand still.

The old man was crafty and false,
  As in this world are many;
He flung his old saddle o'er t' hedge,
  And said, 'Fetch it, if thou'lt have any.'

ghyll] ravine.

59

This thief got off his horse,
  With courage stout and bold,
To search this old man's bags,
  And gave him his horse to hold.

The old man put foot in stirrup,
  And he got on astride;
He set the thief's horse in a gallop,—
  You need not bid the old man ride!

'O, stay! O, stay!' says the thief,
  'And thou half my share shalt have;'
'Nay, marry, not I,' quoth the old man,
  'For once I've bitten a knave!'

This thief he was not content,
  He thought there *must* be bags,
So he up with his rusty sword,
  And chopped the old saddle to rags.

The old man gallop'd and rode,
  Until he was almost spent,
Till he came to his landlord's house,
  And he paid him his whole year's rent

He opened this rogue's portmantle,
  It was glorious for to behold;
There was five hundred pound in money,
  And other five hundred in gold.

His landlord it made him to stare,
  When he did the sight behold;
'Where did thou get the white money,
  And where get the yellow gold?'

'I met a fond fool by the way,
  I swopped horses, and gave him no boot;
But never mind,' says the old man,
  'I got a fond fool by the foot.'

'But now you're grown cramped and old,
   Nor fit for to travel about;'
'O, never mind,' says the old man,
   'I can give these old bones a route!'

As he was a-riding hame,
   And a-down a narrow lane,
He spied his mare tied to a tree,
   And said, 'Tib, thou'lt now gae hame.'

And when that he got hame,
   And told his old wife what he'd done:
She rose and she donned her clothes,
   And about the house did run.

She sung, and she danced, and sung,
   And she sung with a merry devotion,
'If ever our daughter gets wed,
   It will help to enlarge her portion!'

Robin Hood and Little John

When Robin Hood was about twenty years old,
   With a hey down down and a down,
   He happen'd to meet Little John,
A jolly brisk blade, right fit for the trade,
   For he was a lusty young man.

Tho' he was call'd Little, his limbs they were large,
   And his stature was seven foot high;
Wherever he came, they quak'd at his name,
   For soon he would make them to fly.

How they came acquainted, I'll tell you in brief,
   If you will but listen a while;
For this very jest, amongst all the rest,
   I think it may cause you to smile.

Bold Robin Hood said to his jolly bowmen,
  'Pray tarry you here in this grove;
And see that you all observe well my call,
  While thorough the forest I rove.

'We have had no sport for these fourteen long days,
  Therefore now abroad will I go;
Now should I be beat, and cannot retreat,
  My horn I will presently blow.'

Then did he shake hands with his merry men all,
  And bid them at present good-bye;
Then, as near a brook his journey he took,
  A stranger he chanc'd to espy.

They happen'd to meet on a long narrow bridge,
  And neither of them would give way;
Quoth bold Robin Hood, and sturdily stood,
  'I'll show you right Nottingham play.'

With that from his quiver an arrow he drew,
  A broad arrow with a goose-wing:
The stranger replied, 'I'll liquor thy hide,
  If thou offer'st to touch the string.'

Quoth bold Robin Hood, 'Thou dost prate like an ass,
  For were I to bend but my bow,
I could send a dart quite thro' thy proud heart,
  Before thou couldst strike me one blow.'

'Thou talkst like a coward,' the stranger replied;
  'Well arm'd with a long bow you stand,
To shoot at my breast, while I, I protest,
  Have nought but a staff in my hand.'

'The name of a coward,' quoth Robin, 'I scorn,
  Wherefore my long bow I'll lay by;
And now, for thy sake, a staff will I take,
  The truth of thy manhood to try.'

Then Robin Hood stept to a thicket of trees,
  And chose him a staff of ground-oak;
Now this being done, away he did run
  To the stranger, and merrily spoke:

'Lo! see my staff, it is lusty and tough,
  Now here on the bridge we will play;
Whoever falls in, the other shall win
  The battle, and so we'll away,'

'With all my whole heart,' the stranger replied;
  'I scorn in the least to give out;'
This said, they fell to't without more dispute,
  And their staffs they did flourish about.

And first Robin he gave the stranger a bang,
  So hard that it made his bones ring;
The stranger he said, 'This must be repaid,
  I'll give you as good as you bring.'

'So long as I'm able to handle my staff,
  To die in your debt, friend, I scorn:'
Then to it each goes, and follow'd their blows,
  As if they had been threshing of corn.

The stranger gave Robin a crack on the crown,
  Which causèd the blood to appear;
Then Robin, enrag'd, more fiercely engag'd,
  And follow'd his blows more severe.

So thick and so fast did he lay it on him,
  With a passionate fury and ire,
At every stroke, he made him to smoke,
  As if he had been all on fire.

O then into fury the stranger he grew,
  And gave him a damnable look,
And with it a blow that laid him full low,
  And tumbled him into the brook.

'I prithee, good fellow, O where art thou now?'
　The stranger, in laughter, he cried;
Quoth bold Robin Hood, 'Good faith, in the flood,
　And floating along with the tide.'

'I needs must acknowledge thou art a brave soul;
　With thee I'll no longer contend;
For needs must I say, thou hast got the day,
　Our battle shall be at an end.'

Then unto the bank he did presently wade,
　And pull'd himself out by a thorn;
Which done, at the last, he blew a loud blast
　Straitway on his fine bugle-horn.

The echo of which through the valleys did fly,
　At which his stout bowmen appear'd,
All clothèd in green, most gay to be seen;
　So up to their master they steer'd.

'O what's the matter?' quoth William Stutely;
　'Good master, you are wet to the skin:'
'No matter,' quoth he; 'the lad which you see,
　In fighting, hath tumbled me in.'

'He shall not go scot-free,' the others replied;
　So strait they were seizing him there,
To duck him likewise; but Robin Hood cries,
　'He is a stout fellow, forbear.'

'There's no one shall wrong thee, friend, be not afraid;
　These bowmen upon me do wait;
There's threescore and nine; if thou wilt be mine,
　Thou shalt have my livery strait.

'And other accoutrements fit for a man;
　Speak up, jolly blade, never fear;
I'll teach you also the use of the bow,
　To shoot at the fat fallow-deer.'

'O here is my hand,' the stranger reply'd,
   'I'll serve you with all my whole heart;
My name is John Little, a man of good mettle;
   Ne'er doubt me, for I'll play my part.'

'His name shall be alter'd,' quoth William Stutely,
   'And I will his godfather be;
Prepare then a feast, and none of the least,
   For we will be merry,' quoth he.

They presently fetch'd in a brace of fat does,
   With humming strong liquor likewise;
They lov'd what was good; so, in the greenwood,
   This pretty sweet babe they baptize.

He was, I must tell you, but seven foot high,
   And, may be, an ell in the waist;
A pretty sweet lad; much feasting they had;
   Bold Robin the christning graced.

With all his bowmen, which stood in a ring,
   And were of the Nottingham breed;
Brave Stutely comes then, with seven yeomen,
   And did in this manner proceed.

'This infant was called John Little,' quoth he,
   'Which name shall be changèd anon;
The words we'll transpose, so wherever he goes,
   His name shall be call'd Little John.'

They all with a shout made the elements ring,
   So soon as the office was o'er;
To feasting they went, with true merriment,
   And tippled strong liquor galore.

Then Robin he took the pretty sweet babe,
   And clothed him from top to the toe
In garments of green, most gay to be seen,
   And gave him a curious long bow.

'Thou shalt be an archer as well as the best
    And range in the greenwood with us;
Where we'll not want gold nor silver, behold,
    While bishops have aught in their purse.

'We live here like squires, or lords of renown,
    Without e'er a foot of free land;
We feast on good cheer, with wine, ale, and beer,
    And every thing at our command.'

Then music and dancing did finish the day;
    At length, when the sun waxèd low,
Then all the whole train the grove did refrain,
    And unto their caves they did go.

And so ever after, as long as he liv'd,
    Altho' he was proper and tall,
Yet nevertheless, the truth to express,
    Still Little John they did him call.

Robin Hood and the Widow's Three Sons

There are twelve months in all the year,
    As I hear many men say,
But the merriest month in all the year
    Is the merry month of May.

Now Robin Hood is to Nottingham gone,
    With a link a down and a day,
And there he met a silly old woman,
    Was weeping on the way.

'What news? what news, thou silly old woman?
    What news hast thou for me?'
Said she, 'There's three squires in Nottingham town
    To-day is condemn'd to die.'

'O have they parishes burnt?' he said,
    'Or have they ministers slain?
Or have they robb'd any virgin,
    Or other men's wives have ta'en?'—

'They have no parishes burnt, good sir,
　Nor yet have ministers slain,
Nor have they robbed any virgin,
　Nor other men's wives have ta'en.'

'O what have they done?' said bold Robin Hood,
　'I pray thee tell to me.'—
'It's for slaying of the King's fallow deer,
　Bearing their long bows with thee.'—

'Dost thou not mind, old woman,' he said,
　'Since thou made me sup and dine?
By the truth of my body,' quoth bold Robin Hood,
　'You could tell it in no better time.'

Now Robin Hood is to Nottingham gone,
　With a link a down and a day,
And there he met with a silly old palmer,
　Was walking along the highway.

'What news? what news, thou silly old man?
　What news, I do thee pray?'—
Said he, 'Three squires in Nottingham town
　Are condemned to die this day.'—

'Come change thy apparel with me, old man,
　Come change thy apparel for mine;
Here is forty shillings in good silver,
　Go drink it in beer or wine.'—

'O thine apparel is good,' he said,
　'And mine is ragged and torn;
Wherever you go, wherever you ride,
　Laugh ne'er an old man to scorn.'—

'Come change thy apparel with me, old churl,
　Come change thy apparel with mine;
Here are twenty pieces of good broad gold,
　Go feast thy brethren with wine.'

Then he put on the old man's hat,
  It stood full high on the crown:
'The first bold bargain that I come at,
  It shall make thee come down.'

Then he put on the old man's cloak,
  Was patch'd black, blue, and red;
He thought no shame, all the day long,
  To wear the bags of bread.

Then he puts on the old man's breeks,
  Was patch'd from front to side;
'By the truth of my body,' bold Robin can say,
  'This man lov'd little pride!'

Then he put on the old man's hose,
  Were patch'd from knee to wrist;
'By the truth of my body,' said bold Robin Hood,
  'I'd laugh if I had any list.'

Then he put on the old man's shoes,
  Were patch'd both beneath and aboon;
Then Robin Hood swore a solemn oath,
  'It's good habit that makes a man!'

Now Robin Hood is to Nottingham gone,
  With a link a down and a down,
And there he met with the proud Sheriff,
  Was walking along the town.

'O save, O save, O Sheriff,' he said,
  'O save, and you may see!
And what will you give to a silly old man
  To-day will your hangman be?'

'Some suits, some suits,' the Sheriff he said,
  'Some suits I'll give to thee;
Some suits, some suits, and pence thirteen
  To-day's a hangman's fee.'

list] desire for it.

Then Robin he turns him round about,
  And jumps from stock to stone;
'By the truth of my body,' the Sheriff he said,
  'That's well jumpt, thou nimble old man.'—

'I was ne'er a hangman in all my life,
  Nor yet intends to trade;
But curst be he,' said bold Robin,
  'That first a hangman was made!

'I've a bag for meal, and a bag for malt,
  And a bag for barley and corn;
A bag for bread, and a bag for beef,
  And a bag for my little small horn.

'I have a horn in my pockèt,
  I got it from Robin Hood,
And still when I set it to my mouth,
  For thee it blows little good.'—

'O wind thy horn, thou proud fellòw,
  Of thee I have no doubt;
I wish that thou give such a blast
  Till both thy eyes fall out.'

The first loud blast that he did blow,
  He blew both loud and shrill;
A hundred and fifty of Robin Hood's men
  Came riding over the hill.

The next loud blast that he did give,
  He blew both loud and amain;
And quickly sixty of Robin Hood's men
  Came shining over the plain.

'O who are yon,' the Sheriff he said,
  'Come tripping over the lee?'
'They're my attendants,' brave Robin did say,
  'They'll pay a visit to thee.'

They took the gallows from the slack,
    They set it in the glen,
They hang'd the proud Sheriff on that,
    And releas'd their own three men.

slack] hollow.

The Pied Piper of Hamelin
(WRITTEN FOR, AND INSCRIBED TO, W. M. THE YOUNGER)

I

Hamelin Town's in Brunswick,
By famous Hanover city;
    The river Weser, deep and wide,
    Washes its wall on the southern side;
    A pleasanter spot you never spied;
But, when begins my ditty,
    Almost five hundred years ago,
    To see the townsfolk suffer so
      From vermin, was a pity.

II

Rats!
They fought the dogs, and killed the cats,
    And bit the babies in the cradles,
And ate the cheeses out of the vats,
    And licked the soup from the cooks' own ladles,
Split open the kegs of salted sprats,
Made nests inside men's Sunday hats,
And even spoiled the women's chats,
    By drowning their speaking
    With shrieking and squeaking
In fifty different sharps and flats.

III

At last the people in a body
    To the Town Hall came flocking:
"'Tis clear,' cried they, 'our Mayor's a noddy;
    And as for our Corporation—shocking

70

To think we buy gowns lined with ermine
For dolts that can't or won't determine
What's best to rid us of our vermin!
You hope, because you're old and obese,
To find in the furry civic robe ease?
Rouse up, Sirs! Give your brains a racking
To find the remedy we're lacking,
Or, sure as fate, we'll send you packing!'
At this the Mayor and Corporation
Quaked with a mighty consternation.

IV

An hour they sate in council,
   At length the Mayor broke silence:
'For a guilder I'd my ermine gown sell;
   I wish I were a mile hence!
It's easy to bid one rack one's brain—
I'm sure my poor head aches again
I've scratched it so, and all in vain.
Oh for a trap, a trap, a trap!'
Just as he said this, what should hap
At the chamber door but a gentle tap?
'Bless us,' cried the Mayor, 'what's that?'
(With the Corporation as he sat,
Looking little though wondrous fat;
Nor brighter was his eye, nor moister
Than a too-long-opened oyster,
Save when at noon his paunch grew mutinous
For a plate of turtle green and glutinous.)
'Only a scraping of shoes on the mat?
Anything like the sound of a rat
Makes my heart go pit-a-pat!'

V

'Come in!'—the Mayor cried, looking bigger:
And in did come the strangest figure!
His queer long coat from heel to head
Was half of yellow and half of red;

And he himself was tall and thin,
With sharp blue eyes, each like a pin,
And light loose hair, yet swarthy skin,
No tuft on cheek nor beard on chin,
But lips where smiles went out and in—
There was no guessing his kith and kin!
And nobody could enough admire
The tall man and his quaint attire:
Quoth one: 'It's as my great-grandsire,
Starting up at the Trump of Doom's tone,
Had walked this way from his painted tomb-stone!'

VI

He advanced to the council-table:
And, 'Please your honours,' said he, 'I'm able,
By means of a secret charm, to draw
All creatures living beneath the sun,
That creep or swim or fly or run,
After me so as you never saw!
And I chiefly use my charm
On creatures that do people harm,
The mole and toad and newt and viper;
And people call me the Pied Piper.'
(And here they noticed round his neck
A scarf of red and yellow stripe,
To match with his coat of the self-same cheque;
And at the scarf's end hung a pipe;
And his fingers, they noticed, were ever straying
As if impatient to be playing
Upon this pipe, as low it dangled
Over his vesture so old-fangled.)
'Yet,' said he, 'poor piper as I am,
In Tartary I freed the Cham,
Last June, from his huge swarms of gnats;
I eased in Asia the Nizam
Of a monstrous brood of vampyre bats:
And as for what your brain bewilders,
If I can rid your town of rats

Will you give me a thousand guilders?'
'One? fifty thousand!'—was the exclamation
Of the astonished Mayor and Corporation.

VII

Into the street the Piper stept,
  Smiling first a little smile,
As if he knew what magic slept
  In his quiet pipe the while;
Then, like a musical adept,
To blow the pipe his lips he wrinkled,
And green and blue his sharp eyes twinkled
Like a candle-flame where salt is sprinkled;
And ere three shrill notes the pipe uttered,
You heard as if an army muttered;
And the muttering grew to a grumbling;
And the grumbling grew to a mighty rumbling;
And out of the houses the rats came tumbling.
Great rats, small rats, lean rats, brawny rats,
Brown rats, black rats, grey rats, tawny rats,
Grave old plodders, gay young friskers,
    Fathers, mothers, uncles, cousins,
Cocking tails and pricking whiskers,
    Families by tens and dozens,
Brothers, sisters, husbands, wives—
Followed the Piper for their lives.
From street to street he piped advancing,
And step for step they followed dancing,
Until they came to the river Weser
Wherein all plunged and perished!
—Save one who, stout as Julius Caesar,
Swam across and lived to carry
(As he, the manuscript he cherished)
To Rat-land home his commentary:
Which was, 'At the first shrill notes of the pipe,
I heard a sound as of scraping tripe,
And putting apples, wondrous ripe,
Into a cider-press's gripe:

73

And a moving away of pickle-tub-boards,
And a leaving ajar of conserve-cupboards,
And a drawing the corks of train-oil-flasks,
And a breaking the hoops of butter-casks;
And it seemed as if a voice
(Sweeter far than by harp or by psaltery
Is breathed) called out, Oh rats, rejoice!
The world is grown to one vast drysaltery!
So, munch on, crunch on, take your nuncheon,
Breakfast, supper, dinner, luncheon!
And just as a bulky sugar-puncheon,
All ready staved, like a great sun shone
Glorious scarce an inch before me,
Just as methought it said, Come, bore me!
—I found the Weser rolling o'er me.'

VIII

You should have heard the Hamelin people
Ringing the bells till they rocked the steeple.
'Go,' cried the Mayor, 'and get long poles!
Poke out the nests and block up the holes!
Consult with carpenters and builders,
And leave in our town not even a trace
Of the rats!'—when suddenly, up the face
Of the Piper perked in the market-place,
With a 'First, if you please, my thousand guilders!'

IX

A thousand guilders! The Mayor looked blue;
So did the Corporation too.
For council dinners made rare havoc
With Claret, Moselle, Vin-de-Grave, Hock;
And half the money would replenish
Their cellar's biggest butt with Rhenish.
To pay this sum to a wandering fellow
With a gipsy coat of red and yellow!
'Beside,' quoth the Mayor with a knowing wink,
'Our business was done at the river's brink;

We saw with our eyes the vermin sink,
And what's dead can't come to life, I think.
So, friend, we're not the folks to shrink
From the duty of giving you something for drink,
And a matter of money to put in your poke;
But as for the guilders, what we spoke
Of them, as you very well know, was in joke.
Beside, our losses have made us thrifty.
A thousand guilders! Come, take fifty!'

X

The piper's face fell, and he cried,
'No trifling! I can't wait, beside!
I've promised to visit by dinner time
Bagdad, and accept the prime
Of the Head-Cook's pottage, all he's rich in,
For having left, in the Caliph's kitchen,
Of a nest of scorpions no survivor—
With him I proved no bargain-driver,
With you, don't think I'll bate a stiver!
And folks who put me in a passion
May find me pipe to another fashion.'

XI

'How?' cried the Mayor, 'd'ye think I'll brook
Being worse treated than a Cook?
Insulted by a lazy ribald
With idle pipe and vesture piebald?
You threaten us, fellow? Do your worst,
Blow your pipe there till you burst!'

XII

Once more he stept into the street;
    And to his lips again
    Laid his long pipe of smooth straight cane;
And ere he blew three notes (such sweet
Soft notes as yet musician's cunning
Never gave the enraptured air)

75

There was a rustling, that seemed like a bustling
Of merry crowds justling at pitching and hustling,
Small feet were pattering, wooden shoes clattering,
Little hands clapping and little tongues chattering,
And, like fowls in a farm-yard when barley is scattering,
Out came the children running.
All the little boys and girls,
With rosy cheeks and flaxen curls,
And sparkling eyes and teeth like pearls,
Tripping and skipping, ran merrily after
The wonderful music with shouting and laughter.

XIII

The Mayor was dumb, and the Council stood
As if they were changed into blocks of wood,
Unable to move a step, or cry
To the children merrily skipping by—
And could only follow with the eye
That joyous crowd at the Piper's back.
But how the Mayor was on the rack,
And the wretched Council's bosoms beat,
As the Piper turned from the High Street
To where the Weser rolled its waters
Right in the way of their sons and daughters!
However he turned from South to West,
And to Koppelberg Hill his steps addressed,
And after him the children pressed;
Great was the joy in every breast.
'He never can cross that mighty top!
He's forced to let the piping drop,
And we shall see our children stop!'
When, lo, as they reached the mountain's side,
A wondrous portal opened wide,
As if a cavern had suddenly hollowed;
And the Piper advanced and the children followed,
And when all were in to the very last,
The door in the mountain-side shut fast.
Did I say all? No! One was lame,

76

And could not dance the whole of the way;
And in after years, if you would blame
His sadness, he was used to say,—
'It's dull in our town since my playmates left!
I can't forget that I'm bereft
Of all the pleasant sights they see,
Which the Piper also promised me.
For he led us, he said, to a joyous land,
Joining the town and just at hand,
Where waters gushed and fruit-trees grew,
And flowers put forth a fairer hue,
And everything was strange and new;
The sparrows were brighter than peacocks here,
And their dogs outran our fallow deer,
And honey-bees had lost their stings,
And horses were born with eagles' wings:
And just as I became assured
My lame foot would be speedily cured,
The music stopped and I stood still,
And found myself outside the Hill,
Left alone against my will,
To go now limping as before,
And never hear of that country more!'

XIV

Alas, alas for Hamelin!
    There came into many a burgher's pate
    A text which says, that Heaven's Gate
    Opes to the Rich at as easy rate
As the needle's eye takes the camel in!
The Mayor sent East, West, North and South,
To offer the Piper, by word of mouth,
    Wherever it was men's lot to find him,
Silver and gold to his heart's content,
If he'd only return the way he went,
    And bring the children behind him.
But when they saw 'twas a lost endeavour,
And Piper and dancers were gone for ever,

They made a decree that lawyers never
   Should think their records dated duly
If, after the day of the month and year,
These words did not as well appear,
'And so long after what happened here
   On the Twenty-second of July,
Thirteen hundred and seventy-six':
And better in memory to fix
The place of the children's last retreat,
They called it the Pied Piper's Street—
Where any one playing on pipe or tabor
Was sure for the future to lose his labour.
Nor suffered they hostelry or tavern
   To shock with mirth a street so solemn;
But opposite the place of the cavern
   They wrote the story on a column,
And on the great Church Window painted
The same, to make the world acquainted
How their children were stolen away;
And there it stands to this very day.
And I must not omit to say
That in Transylvania there's a tribe
Of alien people that ascribe
The outlandish ways and dress
On which their neighbours lay such stress,
To their fathers and mothers having risen
Out of some subterraneous prison
Into which they were trepanned
Long time ago in a mighty band
Out of Hamelin town in Brunswick land,
But how or why, they don't understand.

XV

So, Willy, let me and you be wipers
Of scores out with all men—especially pipers:
And, whether they pipe us free from rats or from mice,
If we've promised them aught, let us keep our promise.
                       ROBERT BROWNING

The Jackdaw of Rheims

The Jackdaw sat on the Cardinal's chair.
Bishop, and abbot, and prior were there;
  Many a monk, and many a friar,
  Many a knight, and many a squire,
With a great many more of lesser degree,—
In sooth a goodly company;
And they served the Lord Primate on bended knee.
  Never, I ween,
  Was a prouder seen,
Read of in books, or dreamt of in dreams,
Than the Cardinal Lord Archbishop of Rheims!

  In and out
  Through the motley rout,
That little Jackdaw kept hopping about;
  Here and there
  Like a dog in a fair,
  Over comfits and cates,
  And dishes and plates,
Cowl and cope, and rochet and pall,
Mitre and crosier! he hopp'd upon all!
  With saucy air,
  He perch'd on the chair
Where, in state, the great Lord Cardinal sat
In the great Lord Cardinal's great red hat;
  And he peer'd in the face
  Of his Lordship's Grace,
With a satisfied look, as if he would say,
'We two are the greatest folks here to-day!'
  And the priests, with awe,
  As such freaks they saw,
Said, 'The Devil must be in that little Jackdaw!'

The feast was over, the board was clear'd,
The flawns and the custards had all disappear'd,
And six little Singing-boys,—dear little souls!
In nice clean faces, and nice white stoles,

Came, in order due,
Two by two,
Marching that grand refectory through!
A nice little boy held a golden ewer,
Emboss'd and fill'd with water, as pure
As any that flows between Rheims and Namur,
Which a nice little boy stood ready to catch
In a fine golden hand-basin made to match.
Two nice little boys, rather more grown,
Carried lavender-water, and eau de Cologne;
And a nice little boy had a nice cake of soap,
Worthy of washing the hands of the Pope.
One little boy more
A napkin bore,
Of the best white diaper, fringed with pink,
And a Cardinal's Hat mark'd in 'permanent ink.'

The great Lord Cardinal turns at the sight
Of these nice little boys dress'd all in white:
From his finger he draws
His costly turquoise;
And, not thinking at all about little Jackdaws,
Deposits it straight
By the side of his plate,
While the nice little boys on his Eminence wait;
Till, when nobody's dreaming of any such thing,
That little Jackdaw hops off with the ring!
There's a cry and a shout,
And a deuce of a rout,
And nobody seems to know what they're about,
But the Monks have their pockets all turn'd inside out.
The Friars are kneeling,
And hunting, and feeling
The carpet, the floor, and the walls, and the ceiling.
The Cardinal drew
Off each plum-colour'd shoe,
And left his red stockings exposed to the view;
He peeps, and he feels
In the toes and the heels;

They turn up the dishes,—they turn up the plates,—
They take up the poker and poke out the grates,
 —They turn up the rugs,
 They examine the mugs:—
 But, no!—no such thing;—
 They can't find THE RING!
And the Abbot declared that, 'when nobody twigged it,
Some rascal or other had popp'd in, and prigg'd it!'

The Cardinal rose with a dignified look,
He call'd for his candle, his bell, and his book!
 In holy anger, and pious grief,
 He solemnly cursed that rascally thief!
He cursed him at board, he cursed him in bed;
From the sole of his foot to the crown of his head;
He cursed him in sleeping, that every night
He should dream of the devil, and wake in a fright;
He cursed him in eating, he cursed him in drinking,
He cursed him in coughing, in sneezing, in winking;
He cursed him in sitting, in standing, in lying;
He cursed him in walking, in riding, in flying;
He cursed him in living, he cursed him in dying!—
Never was heard such a terrible curse!!
 But what gave rise
 To no little surprise,
Nobody seem'd one penny the worse!
 The day was gone,
 The night came on,
The Monks and the Friars they search'd till dawn;
 When the Sacristan saw,
 On crumpled claw,
Come limping a poor little lame Jackdaw!
 No longer gay,
 As on yesterday;
His feathers all seem'd to be turn'd the wrong way;—
His pinions droop'd—he could hardly stand,—
His head was as bald as the palm of your hand;
 His eye so dim,
 So wasted each limb,

That, heedless of grammar, they all cried, 'THAT'S HIM!—
That's the thief that has got my Lord Cardinal's Ring!'

> The poor little Jackdaw,
> When the Monks he saw,
> Feebly gave vent to the ghost of a caw;
> And turn'd his bald head, as much as to say
> 'Pray, be so good as to walk this way!'
> Slower and slower
> He limp'd on before,
> Till they came to the back of the belfry door,
> Where the first thing they saw,
> Midst the sticks and the straw,
> Was the RING in the nest of that little Jackdaw!

> Then the great Lord Cardinal call'd for his book,
> And off that terrible curse he took;
> The mute expression
> Served in lieu of confession,
> And, being thus coupled with full restitution,
> The Jackdaw got plenary absolution!
> —When those words were heard,
> That poor little bird
> Was so changed in a moment, 'twas really absurd.
> He grew sleek, and fat;
> In addition to that,
> A fresh crop of feathers came thick as a mat.
> His tail waggled more
> Even than before;
> But no longer it wagg'd with an impudent air,
> No longer he perch'd on the Cardinal's chair.
> He hopp'd now about
> With a gait devout;
> At Matins, at Vespers, he never was out;
> And, so far from any more pilfering deeds,
> He always seem'd telling the Confessor's beads.
> If any one lied,—or if any one swore,—
> Or slumber'd in pray'r-time and happen'd to snore,

That good Jackdaw
Would give a great 'Caw!'
As much as to say, 'Don't do so any more!'
While many remark'd, as his manners they saw,
That they 'never had known such a pious Jackdaw!'
    He long lived the pride
    Of that country-side,
And at last in the odour of sanctity died;
    When, as words were too faint
    His merits to paint,
The Conclave determined to make him a Saint;
And on newly made Saints and Popes, as you know,
It's the custom, at Rome, new names to bestow,
So they canonized him by the name of Jim Crow!

R. H. BARHAM

THE POET'S FEELING

We all know what we mean when we say 'I am feeling happy today'. We are in a pleasant state of well-being, and the world seems to be a fine place. When we say that we are unhappy, then life is not so enjoyable.

These are simple and obvious feelings, that of happiness and unhappiness, of pleasure and its opposite.

Again we express our feelings when we say 'What a lovely sunset', or 'Don't these flowers smell sweet'. These are expressions of our feelings of pleasure.

Poets often express their spontaneous feelings of pleasure:

> My heart leaps up when I behold
> A rainbow in the sky,

or

> My heart is like a singing bird
> Whose nest is in a watered shoot.

Sometimes they express the opposite feeling:

> And every spirit upon Earth
> Seemed fervourless as I.

A simple natural feeling may be checked like a flowing stream by all kinds of barriers; this check leads to a more complicated state of feeling called emotion. A feeling of unhappiness may, for many different reasons, turn into fear or anger. These emotions can be very powerful.

When the desires of a child are thwarted, he may give way to a violent burst of anger, screaming and throwing things about. As he grows older he learns to control himself and to express this emotional outburst in words. These may be violent too, or they may be controlled and so used with greater effect.

Poets not only feel far more strongly than most people, but in their poetry they are able to tell us very effectively just how they feel. We may find that the poet writes about feelings that we have experienced ourselves but which we are unable to put into words, and we have a certain pleasure when we see these feelings so vividly realized. When the poet expresses more profound emotional experiences than we have yet had we may, as we read, extend our sympathies by sharing in some part in those experiences, from the expression of joy to an outburst of anger:

> And he and they together
> Knelt down with angry prayers
> For tamed and shabby tigers,
> And dancing dogs and bears...

or of grief:

> But down in my garden forsaken, forsaken
> I'll weep all the day by my red fuchsia tree!

The Rainbow

> My heart leaps up when I behold
>   A rainbow in the sky:
> So was it when my life began;
> So is it now I am a man;
> So be it when I shall grow old,
>   Or let me die!
> The Child is father of the Man;
> And I could wish my days to be
> Bound each to each by natural piety.
>
> WILLIAM WORDSWORTH

85

A Great Time

Sweet Chance, that led my steps abroad,
  Beyond the town, where wild flowers grow—
A rainbow and a cuckoo, Lord,
  How rich and great the times are now!
    Know, all ye sheep
    And cows, that keep
On staring that I stand so long
  In grass that's wet from heavy rain—
A rainbow and a cuckoo's song
  May never come together again;
    May never come
    This side the tomb.   W. H. DAVIES

The Fiddler of Dooney

When I play on my fiddle in Dooney
Folk dance like a wave of the sea;
My cousin is priest in Kilvarnet,
My brother in Moharabuiee.

I pass'd my brother and cousin:
They read in their books of prayer;
I read in my book of songs
I bought at the Sligo fair.

When we come at the end of time,
To Peter sitting in state,
He will smile on the three old spirits,
But call me first through the gate;

For the good are always the merry,
Save by an evil chance;
And the merry love the fiddle,
And the merry love to dance:

And when the folk there spy me,
They will all come up to me,
With 'Here is the fiddler of Dooney!'
And dance like a wave of the sea.   W. B. YEATS

86

A Birthday

My heart is like a singing bird
  Whose nest is in a watered shoot;
My heart is like an apple-tree
  Whose boughs are bent with thick-set fruit;
My heart is like a rainbow shell
  That paddles in a halcyon sea;
My heart is gladder than all these,
  Because my love is come to me.

Raise me a dais of silk and down;
  Hang it with vair and purple dyes;
Carve it in doves and pomegranates,
  And peacocks with a hundred eyes;
Work it in gold and silver grapes,
  In leaves, and silver fleurs-de-lys;
Because the birthday of my life
  Is come, my love is come to me.

CHRISTINA ROSSETTI

To the Cuckoo

O blithe New-comer! I have heard,
  I hear thee and rejoice:
O Cuckoo! shall I call thee Bird,
  Or but a wandering Voice?

While I am lying on the grass
  Thy twofold shout I hear;
From hill to hill it seems to pass,
  At once far off and near.

Though babbling only to the vale
  Of sunshine and of flowers,
Thou bringest unto me a tale
  Of visionary hours.

Thrice welcome, darling of the Spring!
    Even yet thou art to me
No bird, but an invisible thing,
    A voice, a mystery;

The same whom in my school-boy days
    I listen'd to; that Cry
Which made me look a thousand ways
    In bush, and tree, and sky,

To seek thee did I often rove
    Through woods and on the green;
And thou wert still a hope, a love;
    Still long'd for, never seen!

And I can listen to thee yet;
    Can lie upon the plain
And listen, till I do beget
    That golden time again.

O blessèd Bird! the earth we pace
    Again appears to be
An unsubstantial, faery place,
    That is fit home for Thee!

            WILLIAM WORDSWORTH

The Darkling Thrush

I leant upon a coppice gate
    When Frost was spectre-gray,
And Winter's dregs made desolate
    The weakening eye of day.
The tangled bine-stems scored the sky
    Like strings of broken lyres,
And all mankind that haunted nigh
    Had sought their household fires.

The land's sharp features seemed to be
    The Century's corpse outleant,
His crypt the cloudy canopy,
    The wind his death-lament.

88

The ancient pulse of germ and birth
  Was shrunken hard and dry,
And every spirit upon earth
  Seemed fervourless as I.

At once a voice arose among
  The bleak twigs overhead
In a full-hearted evensong
  Of joy illimited;
An aged thrush, frail, gaunt, and small,
  In blast-beruffled plume,
Has chosen thus to fling his soul
  Upon the growing gloom.

So little cause for carollings
  Of such ecstatic sound
Was written on terrestrial things
  Afar or nigh around,
That I could think there trembled through
  His happy good-night air
Some blessèd Hope, whereof he knew
  And I was unaware.   THOMAS HARDY

The Vagabond

Give to me the life I love,
  Let the lave go by me,
Give the jolly heaven above
  And the byway nigh me.
Bed in the bush with stars to see,
  Bread I dip in the river—
There's the life for a man like me,
  There's the life for ever.

Let the blow fall soon or late,
  Let what will be o'er me;
Give the face of earth around
  And the road before me.

Wealth I seek not, hope nor love,
    Nor a friend to know me;
All I seek, the heaven above,
    And the road below me.

Or let autumn fall on me
    Where afield I linger,
Silencing the bird on tree,
    Biting the blue finger.
White as meal the frosty field—
    Warm the fireside haven—
Not to autumn will I yield,
    Not to winter even!

Let the blow fall soon or late.
    Let what will be o'er me;
Give the face of earth around,
    And the road before me.
Wealth I ask not, hope nor love,
    Nor a friend to know me;
All I ask, the heaven above,
    And the road below me.

ROBERT LOUIS STEVENSON

An Old Woman of the Roads

Oh, to have a little house!
    To own the hearth and stool and all!
The heaped-up sods upon the fire,
    The pile of turf against the wall!

To have a clock with weights and chains
    And pendulum swinging up and down!
A dresser filled with shining delph,
    Speckled and white and blue and brown!

I could be busy all the day
    Clearing and sweeping hearth and floor,
And fixing on their shelf again
    My white and blue and speckled store!

I could be quiet there at night
  Beside the fire and by myself,
Sure of a bed, and loth to leave
  The ticking clock and the shining delph!

Och! but I'm weary of mist and dark,
  And roads where there's never a house or bush,
And tired I am of bog and road
  And the crying wind and the lonesome hush!

And I am praying to God on high,
  And I am praying Him night and day,
For a little house—a house of my own—
  Out of the wind's and the rain's way.

PADRAIC COLUM

Sea Fever

I must go down to the seas again, to the lonely sea and the sky,
And all I ask is a tall ship, and a star to steer her by;
And the wheel's kick and the wind's song and the white sail's shaking,
And the grey mist on the sea's face, and a grey dawn breaking.

I must go down to the seas again, for the call of the running tide
Is a wild call and a clear call that may not be denied;
And all I ask is a windy day with the white clouds flying,
And the flung spray and the blown spume, and the seagulls crying.

I must go down to the seas again, to the vagrant gipsy life,
To the gull's way and the whale's way where the wind's like a
    whetted knife;
And all I ask is a merry yarn from a laughing fellow-rover,
And a quiet sleep and a sweet dream when the long trick's over.

JOHN MASEFIELD

The Lake Isle of Innisfree

I will arise and go now, and go to Innisfree,
And a small cabin build there, of clay and wattles made;
Nine bean rows will I have there, a hive for the honey-bee,
And live alone in the bee-loud glade.

And I shall have some peace there, for peace comes dropping slow,
Dropping from the veils of the morning to where the cricket sings;
There midnight's all a-glimmer, and noon a purple glow,
And evening full of the linnet's wings.

I will arise and go now, for always night and day
I hear lake water lapping with low sounds by the shore;
While I stand on the roadway, or on the pavements gray,
I hear it in the deep heart's core.   W. B. YEATS

The Lamb

Little Lamb, who made thee?
Dost thou know who made thee?
Gave thee life, and bid thee feed,
By the stream and o'er the mead;
Gave thee clothing of delight,
Softest clothing, woolly, bright;
Gave thee such a tender voice,
Making all the vales rejoice?
Little Lamb, who made thee?
Dost thou know who made thee?

Little Lamb, I'll tell thee,
Little Lamb, I'll tell thee:
He is callèd by thy name,
For He calls Himself a Lamb.
He is meek, and He is mild;
He became a little child.
I a child, and thou a lamb,
We are callèd by His name.
Little Lamb, God bless thee!
Little Lamb, God bless thee!

WILLIAM BLAKE

The Tyger

Tyger! Tyger! burning bright
In the forests of the night,
What immortal hand or eye
Could frame thy fearful symmetry?

In what distant deeps or skies
Burnt the fire of thine eyes?
On what wings dare he aspire?
What the hand dare seize the fire?

And what shoulder, and what art,
Could twist the sinews of thy heart?
And when thy heart began to beat,
What dread hand? and what dread feet?

What the hammer? what the chain?
In what furnace was thy brain?
What the anvil? what dread grasp
Dare its deadly terrors clasp?

When the stars threw down their spears,
And water'd heaven with their tears,
Did He smile His work to see?
Did He who made the Lamb make thee?

Tyger! Tyger! burning bright
In the forests of the night,
What immortal hand or eye,
Dare frame thy fearful symmetry?

WILLIAM BLAKE

To a Black Greyhound

Shining black in the shining light,
  Inky black in the golden sun,
Graceful as the swallow's flight,
  Light as swallow, wingèd one,
Swift as driven hurricane—
  Double-sinewed stretch and spring,
Muffled thud of flying feet,
  See the black dog galloping,
  Hear his wild foot-beat.

See him lie when the day is dead,
  Black curves curled on the boarded floor.
Sleepy eyes, my sleepy-head—
  Eyes that were aflame before.
Gentle now, they burn no more;
  Gentle now and softly warm,
With the fire that made them bright
  Hidden—as when after storm
Softly falls the night.

God of speed, who makes the fire—
  God of Peace, who lulls the same—
God who gives the fierce desire,
  Lust for blood as fierce as flame—
God who stands in Pity's name—
  Many may ye be or less,
Ye who rule the earth and sun:
  Gods of strength and gentleness
  Ye are ever one.   JULIAN GRENFELL

The Dromedary

In dreams I see the Dromedary still,
  As once in a gay park I saw him stand:
  A thousand eyes in vulgar wonder scanned
His humps and hairy neck, and gazed their fill
At his lank shanks and mocked with laughter shrill.
  He never moved: and if his Eastern land
  Flashed on his eye with stretches of hot sand,
It wrung no mute appeal from his proud will.
He blinked upon the rabble lazily;
  And still some trace of majesty forlorn
And a coarse grace remained: his head was high,
  Though his gaunt flanks with a great mange were worn:
There was not any yearning in his eye,
  But on his lips and nostril infinite scorn.
                                      A. Y. CAMPBELL

The Bells of Heaven

'Twould ring the bells of Heaven
The wildest peal for years,
If Parson lost his senses
And people came to theirs,
And he and they together
Knelt down with angry prayers
For tamed and shabby tigers,
And dancing dogs and bears,
And wretched, blind pit ponies,
And little hunted hares.   RALPH HODGSON

Stupidity Street

I saw with open eyes
Singing birds sweet
Sold in the shops
For the people to eat,
Sold in the shops of
Stupidity Street.

I saw in vision
The worm in the wheat,
And in the shops nothing
For people to eat;
Nothing for sale in
Stupidity Street.   RALPH HODGSON

The Snare

I hear a sudden cry of pain!
There is a rabbit in a snare:
Now I hear the cry again,
But I cannot tell from where.

But I cannot tell from where
He is calling out for aid!
Crying on the frightened air,
Making everything afraid!

Making everything afraid!
Wrinkling up his little face!
And he cries again for aid;
And I cannot find the place!

And I cannot find the place
Where his paw is in the snare!
Little One! Oh, Little One!
I am searching everywhere!

JAMES STEPHENS

O What if the Fowler

O what if the fowler my blackbird has taken?
　The roses of dawn blossom over the sea;
Awaken, my blackbird, awaken, awaken,
　And sing to me out of my red fuchsia tree!

O what if the fowler my blackbird has taken?
　The sun lifts his head from the lap of the sea—
Awaken, my blackbird, awaken, awaken,
　And sing to me out of my red fuchsia tree!

O what if the fowler my blackbird has taken?
　The mountain grows white with the birds of the sea;
But down in my garden forsaken, forsaken,
　I'll weep all the day by my red fuchsia tree!

CHARLES DALMON

PART II

THE POET'S SONG

If we like dancing we are usually fond of music also; and music has played a great part in the story of man.

In court circles in Elizabeth I's time, music was considered to be as essential a part of education as reading and writing. Queen Elizabeth I herself was an excellent performer on the virginals, an instrument with a small keyboard like a piano. One was expected to be able to read music, play an instrument, and join in a madrigal. These part-songs were usually light-hearted, very often sung in praise of the Queen. There was a great demand for words to go with the music, and educated people wrote songs for music as readily as they wrote music for the songs. We have not only songs at court and in the great houses of the aristocracy, but in taverns, at fair-grounds, and in the theatre.

The songs in Shakespeare's plays were all written to be sung, and would be another source of pleasure to his audience, who delighted in music. When we read, today, such songs as:

Come unto these yellow sands

we are conscious of the music of the words themselves; the sound and rhythm of the lines have a delicate and individual movement which can be appreciated quite apart from the musical accompaniment.

Listen to these lines:

It was a lover and his lass,
   With a hey, and a ho, and a hey nonino,
That o'er the green corn-field did pass,

99

In the spring time, the only pretty ring time,
When birds do sing, hey ding a ding, ding;
Sweet lovers love the spring.

The sound of such a poem pleases the ear so much that it would be printed not for singing but for reading and that is lyrical poetry.

This separation from music gave the lyric greater freedom and a wider range. Songs were mostly on the subject of love, which was treated in a conventional, rather artificial way, with ready-made epithets and phrases. Lovers were often called shepherds and they piped on oaten straws. The lady's lips were cherries, her eyes were like stars, and her teeth were pearls.

Now came a change from such flattering love songs. The lyric became a simple expression of wonder, joy, or sorrow in words that made their own music: it is gay, careless, and impersonal:

Gather ye rosebuds while ye may,
Old Time is still a-flying:
And this same flower that smiles today
Tomorrow will be dying.

One should not think too closely of the meaning of a lyric, but surrender oneself to the sound, and be moved by that. All great lyrics mean far more than they seem to say—they express something beyond the mere prose sense of the words, so listen carefully to the sound.

Come unto these Yellow Sands

Come unto these yellow sands,
  And then take hands:
Court'sied when you have, and kiss'd,
  The wild waves whist,
Foot it featly here and there;
And, sweet sprites, the burthen bear.
      Hark, hark!
        Bow, wow,
      The watch-dogs bark:
        Bow, wow.
      Hark, hark! I hear
    The strain of strutting chanticleer
    Cry, Cock-a-diddle-dow!
                WILLIAM SHAKESPEARE

Over Hill, Over Dale

Over hill, over dale,
  Thorough bush, thorough brier,
Over park, over pale,
  Thorough flood, thorough fire,
I do wander everywhere,
Swifter than the moonè's sphere;
And I serve the fairy queen,
To dew her orbs upon the green:
The cowslips tall her pensioners be;
In their gold coats spots you see;
Those be rubies, fairy favours,
In those freckles live their savours:
I must go seek some dew-drops here,
And hang a pearl in every cowslip's ear.
                WILLIAM SHAKESPEARE

You Spotted Snakes

You spotted snakes with double tongue,
  Thorny hedgehogs, be not seen;
Newts and blind-worms, do no wrong;
  Come not near our fairy queen.

    Philomel, with melody,
     Sing in our sweet lullaby;
  Lulla, lulla, lullaby; lulla, lulla, lullaby!
      Never harm,
      Nor spell nor charm,
    Come our lovely lady nigh;
    So, good night, with lullaby.

Weaving spiders, come not here;
  Hence, you long-legg'd spinners, hence!
Beetles black, approach not near;
  Worm nor snail, do no offence.

    Philomel, with melody,
     Sing in our sweet lullaby;
  Lulla, lulla, lullaby; lulla, lulla, lullaby!
      Never harm,
      Nor spell nor charm,
    Come our lovely lady nigh;
    So, good night, with lullaby.

              WILLIAM SHAKESPEARE

Where the Bee Sucks

Where the bee sucks, there suck I:
In a cowslip's bell I lie;
There I couch when owls do cry.
On the bat's back I do fly
After summer merrily:
  Merrily, merrily, shall I live now,
  Under the blossom that hangs on the bough.

              WILLIAM SHAKESPEARE

Clock-a-Clay

In the cowslip pips I lie,
Hidden from the buzzing fly,
While green grass beneath me lies,
Pearled with dew like fishes' eyes,
Here I lie, a clock-a-clay,
Waiting for the time of day.

While grassy forest quakes surprise,
And the wild wind sobs and sighs,
My gold home rocks as like to fall,
On its pillar green and tall;
When the pattering rain drives by
Clock-a-clay keeps warm and dry.

Day by day and night by night,
All the week I hide from sight;
In the cowslip pips I lie,
In rain and dew still warm and dry;
Day and night, and night and day
Red, black-spotted clock-a-clay.

My home shakes in wind and showers,
Pale green pillar topped with flowers,
Bending at the wild wind's breath,
Till I touch the grass beneath;
Here I live, lone clock-a-clay,
Watching for the time of day.   JOHN CLARE

clock-a-clay] ladybird.

A Laughing Song

When the green woods laugh with the voice of joy,
And the dimpling stream runs laughing by;
When the air does laugh with our merry wit,
And the green hill laughs with the noise of it;

When the meadows laugh with lively green,
And the grasshopper laughs in the merry scene;
When Mary, and Susan, and Emily,
With their sweet round mouths sing, 'Ha, ha, he!'

When the painted birds laugh in the shade,
Where our table with cherries and nuts is spread:
Come live, and be merry, and join with me
To sing the sweet chorus of 'Ha, ha, he!'

WILLIAM BLAKE

Reeds of Innocence

Piping down the valleys wild,
  Piping songs of pleasant glee,
On a cloud I saw a child,
  And he laughing said to me:

'Pipe a song about a Lamb!'
  So I piped with merry cheer.
'Piper, pipe that song again;'
  So I piped: he wept to hear.

'Drop thy pipe, thy happy pipe;
  Sing thy songs of happy cheer:'
So I sang the same again,
  While he wept with joy to hear.

'Piper, sit thee down and write
  In a book, that all may read.'
So he vanished from my sight,
  And I plucked a hollow reed,

And I made a rural pen,
  And I stained the water clear,
And I wrote my happy songs
  Every child may joy to hear. WILLIAM BLAKE

The Echoing Green

The Sun does arise,
And make happy the skies;
The merry bells ring
To welcome the Spring;

The skylark and thrush,
The birds of the bush,
Sing louder around
To the bells' cheerful sound,
While our sports shall be seen
On the Echoing Green.

Old John, with white hair,
Does laugh away care,
Sitting under the oak,
Among the old folk.
They laugh at our play,
And soon they all say:
'Such, such were the joys
When we all, girls and boys,
In our youth-time were seen
On the Echoing Green.'

Till the little ones, weary,
No more can be merry;
The sun does descend,
And our sports have an end.
Round the laps of their mothers
Many sisters and brothers,
Like birds in their nest,
Are ready for rest,
And sport no more seen
On the darkening Green.   WILLIAM BLAKE

The Fifteen Acres

I

I cling and swing
On a branch, or sing
Through the cool, clear hush of morning, O!

Or fling my wing
On the air, and bring
To sleepier birds a warning, O!

That the night's in flight,
And the sun's in sight,
And the dew is the grass adorning, O!

And the green leaves swing
As I sing, sing, sing,
  Up by the river,
    Down by the dell,
  To the little wee nest
    Where the big tree fell,
  So early in the morning, O!

II

I flit and twit
In the sun for a bit
When his light so bright is shining, O!

Or sit and fit
My plumes, or knit
Straw plaits for the nest's nice lining, O!

And she with glee,
Shows unto me,
Underneath her wings reclining, O!

And I sing that Peg
Has an egg, egg, egg!
  Up by the oat-field,
    Round the mill;
  Past the meadow,
    Down the hill,
  So early in the morning, O!

III

I stoop and swoop
On the air, or loop
Through the trees, and then go soaring, O!

To group, with a troop
On the skiey poop
While the sun behind is roaring, O!

I skim and swim
By the cloud's red rim;
And up to the azure flooring, O!

And my wide wings drip,
As I slip, slip, slip,
  Down through the raindrops,
    Back where Peg
  Broods in the nest
    On the little white egg
So early in the morning, O!

JAMES STEPHENS

The Woodlark

Teevo cheevo cheevio chee:
O where, what can thàt be?
Weedio-weedio:
            There again!
So tiny a trickle of sòng-strain;
And all round not to be found
For brier, bough, furrow, or grèen ground
Before or behind or far or at hand
Either left either right
Anywhere in the sùnlight.
Well, after all! Ah but hark—
'I am the little wòodlark.
The skylark is my cousin and he
Is known to men more than me...
To-day the sky is two and two
With white strokes and strains of the blue.
The blue wheat-acre is underneath
And the braided ear breaks out of the sheath,
The ear in milk, lush the sash,
And crush-silk poppies aflash,
The blood-gush blade-gash
Flame-rash rudred
Bud shelling or broad-shed

107

Tatter-tassel-tangled and dingle-a-dangled
Dandy-hung dainty head.
And down...the furrow dry
Sunspurge and oxeye
And lace-leaved lovely
Foam-tuft fumitory...
Through the velvety wind V-winged
To the nest's nook I balance and buoy
With a sweet joy of a sweet joy,
Sweet, of a sweet, of a sweet joy.
Of a sweet—a sweet—sweet joy.'

GERARD MANLEY HOPKINS

This is not a finished poem, only a collection of fragments. 'The
blood-gush blade-gash' is a description of a half-open poppy bud
and 'rudred' is another form of 'ruddy'.

Blow, Blow, thou Winter Wind

Blow, blow, thou winter wind,
Thou art not so unkind
  As man's ingratitude;
Thy tooth is not so keen,
Because thou art not seen,
  Although thy breath be rude.
Heigh ho! sing, heigh ho! unto the green holly;
Most friendship is feigning, most loving mere folly:
  Then heigh ho, the holly!
  This life is most jolly.

Freeze, freeze, thou bitter sky,
That dost not bite so nigh
  As benefits forgot;
Though thou the waters warp,
Thy sting is not so sharp
  As friend remember'd not.
Heigh ho! sing, heigh ho! unto the green holly;
Most friendship is feigning, most loving mere folly:
  Then heigh ho, the holly!
  This life is most jolly.   WILLIAM SHAKESPEARE

Now the Hungry Lion Roars

Now the hungry lion roars,
  And the wolf behowls the moon;
Whilst the heavy ploughman snores,
  All with weary task fordone.
Now the wasted brands do glow,
  Whilst the scritch-owl, scritching loud,
Puts the wretch that lies in woe
  In remembrance of a shroud.
Now it is the time of night
  That the graves, all gaping wide,
Every one lets forth his sprite,
  In the churchway paths to glide:
And we fairies, that do run
  By the triple Hecate's team
From the presence of the sun,
  Following darkness like a dream,
Now are frolic; not a mouse
Shall disturb this hallowed house:
I am sent with broom before,
To sweep the dust behind the door.

Through the house give glimmering light,
  By the dead and drowsy fire;
Every elf and fairy sprite
  Hop as light as bird from brier;
And this ditty after me
Sing, and dance it trippingly.
First, rehearse your song by rote,
To each word a warbling note:
Hand in hand, with fairy grace,
Will we sing, and bless this place.
Now, until the break of day,
Through this house each fairy stray.
To the best bride-bed will we,
Which by us shall blessed be;
And the issue there create
Ever shall be fortunate.

So shall all the couples three
Ever true in loving be;
And the blots of Nature's hand
Shall not in their issue stand;
Never mole, hare-lip, nor scar,
Nor mark prodigious, such as are
Despisèd in nativity,
Shall upon their children be.
With this field-dew consecrate,
Every fairy take his gait;
And every several chamber bless,
Through this palace with sweet peace:
And the owner of it blest,
Ever shall in safety rest.
   Trip away;
   Make no stay:
Meet me all by break of day.

            WILLIAM SHAKESPEARE

Overheard on a Saltmarsh

Nymph, nymph, what are your beads?
Green glass, goblin. Why do you stare at them?
Give them me.

      No.

Give them me. Give them me.

          No.

Then I will howl all night in the reeds,
Lie in the mud and howl for them.
Goblin, why do you love them so?
They are better than stars or water,
Better than voices of winds that sing,
Better than any man's fair daughter,
Your green glass beads on a silver ring.
Hush, I stole them out of the moon.

Give me your beads, I want them.
                              No.
I will lie and howl in a deep lagoon
For your green glass beads, I love them so.
Give them me. Give them.
                    No.
                              HAROLD MONRO

Full Fathom Five

Full fathom five thy father lies;
    Of his bones are coral made;
Those are pearls that were his eyes:
    Nothing of him that doth fade,
But doth suffer a sea-change
Into something rich and strange.
Sea-nymphs hourly ring his knell:
                              Ding-dong.
    Hark! now I hear them—
                    Ding-dong, bell!
                    WILLIAM SHAKESPEARE

A Dirge

Call for the robin-redbreast and the wren,
Since o'er shady groves they hover,
And with leaves and flowers do cover
The friendless bodies of unburied men.
Call unto his funeral dole
The ant, the field-mouse, and the mole,
To rear him hillocks that shall keep him warm,
And (when gay tombs are robb'd) sustain no harm;
But keep the wolf far thence, that's foe to men,
For with his nails he'll dig them up again.
                    JOHN WEBSTER

The Brook

I come from haunts of coot and hern,
  I make a sudden sally,
And sparkle out among the fern,
  To bicker down a valley.

By thirty hills I hurry down
  Or slip between the ridges,
By twenty thorps, a little town,
  And half a hundred bridges.

Till last by Philip's farm I flow
  To join the brimming river,
For men may come and men may go,
  But I go on for ever.

I chatter over stony ways,
  In little sharps and trebles,
I bubble into eddying bays,
  I babble on the pebbles.

With many a curve my banks I fret,
  By many a field and fallow,
And many a fairy foreland set
  With willow-weed and mallow.

I chatter, chatter, as I flow
  To join the brimming river,
For men may come and men may go,
  But I go on for ever.

I wind about, and in and out,
  With here a blossom sailing,
And here and there a lusty trout,
  And here and there a grayling,

And here and there a foamy flake
  Upon me, as I travel
With many a silvery waterbreak
  Above the golden gravel,

And draw them all along, and flow
  To join the brimming river,
For men may come and men may go,
  But I go on for ever.

I steal by lawns and grassy plots,
  I slide by hazel covers;
I move the sweet forget-me-nots
  That grow for happy lovers.

I slip, I slide, I gloom, I glance,
  Among my skimming swallows;
I make the netted sunbeam dance
  Against my sandy shallows.

I murmur under moon and stars
  In brambly wildernesses;
I linger by my shingly bars;
  I loiter round my cresses;

And out again I curve and flow
  To join the brimming river,
For men may come and men may go,
  But I go on for ever.

LORD TENNYSON

The Shell

And then I pressed the shell
  Close to my ear
And listened well,
And straightway like a bell
  Came low and clear
The slow, sad murmur of far distant seas,
Whipped by an icy breeze
  Upon a shore
Wind-swept and desolate
  It was a sunless strand that never bore
The footprint of a man,
  Nor felt the weight
Since time began

Of any human quality or stir
Save what the dreary winds and waves incur.
And in the hush of waters was the sound
Of pebbles rolling round
For ever rolling with a hollow sound.
And bubbling sea-weeds as the waters go
Swish to and fro
Their long, cold tentacles of slimy grey.
There was no day,
Nor ever came a night
Setting the stars alight
To wonder at the moon:
Was twilight only and the frightened croon,
Smitten to whimpers, of the dreary wind
And waves that journeyed blind—
And then I loosed my ear—oh, it was sweet
To hear a cart go jolting down the street!

JAMES STEPHENS

THE NATURAL SCENE

When we are in a hurry and become excited because our friends are dawdling along, we may call them slow coaches, or tell them they are as slow as snails, or just like a lot of tortoises.

Everyday speech is full of such comparisons. We often use phrases such as: cool as a cucumber, quick as lightning, dead as a door-nail. These express our feelings vividly by calling up a picture.

Poetry is always comparing things; setting two objects side by side so that we may understand each a little better. By comparing we attempt to know. By successfully comparing, as the poet does, we make and announce discovery.

> That is the flycatcher's wing beneath the eaves
> A frivolous quick sound like an opening fan.

The sound of the bird's wing opening is like a fan—this simile (a comparison introduced by *like* or *as*) gives us a vivid picture of the stiff wing feathers suddenly spreading out wide and we hear the dry quick sound. In our imagination we see and hear the wing and the fan at one time.

> The bat...like a glove, a black glove thrown up at the light,
> And falling back.

This is both simple and effective. The glove is a soft, black, shapeless object, and immediately we see the bat as a glove.

> On lawns as smooth as shining glass

is the poet's way of saying the lawns shine with smoothness.

We sometimes say that a person has a sharp tongue. We mean his tongue is like a sharp instrument, it can cut and wound. This metaphor is a compressed simile, a direct identification, and says a great deal in a single word. This concentration of expression is essentially poetic, and you will find that metaphors are common in poetry and give striking, bright pictures in words:

> The cherry and the hoary pear
> Scatter their snow around,

and

The deep sea horses plunging, restless, fretted by the whip of wind
Tugging green tons.

Metaphors, like similes, can describe things heard as well as things seen:

The mallard...stretch out into the wind and sound their horns
 again,

which is the poet's way of saying the mallard stretch out into the wind and utter cries which sound like motor-horns. We may not have heard the cry of wild duck, but we do know the sound of motor-horns, and the two sounds are now brought together in one word.

The poet uses simile and metaphor to describe the world around him. You will notice that a good deal of this description is of the countryside, and particularly of the season, Spring.

From early times the coming of Spring was the most wonderful event of the whole year, the change from the cold, dark, cheerless Winter to warmth and new sparkling life. The intense desire for the coming of Spring compelled men to write of this season, and it is described and praised by generations of poets:

Spring, the sweet Spring, is the year's pleasant king.

Spring

Spring, the sweet Spring, is the year's pleasant king;
Then blooms each thing, then maids dance in a ring,
Cold doth not sting, the pretty birds do sing—
    Cuckoo, jug-jug, pu-we, to-witta-woo!

The palm and may make country houses gay,
Lambs frisk and play, the shepherds pipe all day,
And we hear aye birds tune this merry lay—
    Cuckoo, jug-jug, pu-we, to-witta-woo!

The fields breathe sweet, the daisies kiss our feet,
Young lovers meet, old wives a-sunning sit,
In every street these tunes our ears do greet—
    Cuckoo, jug-jug, pu-we, to-witta-woo!
        Spring, the sweet Spring!

                THOMAS NASHE

Home-thoughts, from Abroad

O to be in England
Now that April's there,
And whoever wakes in England
Sees, some morning, unaware,
That the lowest boughs and the brushwood sheaf
Round the elm-tree bole are in tiny leaf,
While the chaffinch sings on the orchard bough
In England—now!

And after April, when May follows,
And the whitethroat builds, and all the swallows!
Hark, where my blossom'd pear-tree in the hedge
Leans to the field and scatters on the clover
Blossoms and dewdrops—at the bent spray's edge—
That's the wise thrush; he sings each song twice over,
Lest you should think he never could recapture
The first fine careless rapture!

And though the fields look rough with hoary dew,
All will be gay when noontide wakes anew
The buttercups, the little children's dower
—Far brighter than this gaudy melon-flower!

ROBERT BROWNING

Return of Spring

Now fades the last long streak of snow,
  Now burgeons every maze of quick
  About the flowering squares, and thick
By ashen roots the violets blow.

Now rings the woodland loud and long,
  The distance takes a lovelier hue,
  And drown'd in yonder living blue
The lark becomes a sightless song.

Now dance the lights on lawn and lea,
  The flocks are whiter down the vale,
  And milkier every milky sail
On winding stream or distant sea;

Where now the seamew pipes, or dives
  In yonder greening gleam, and fly
  The happy birds, that change their sky
To build and brood; that live their lives

From land to land; and in my breast
  Spring wakens too; and my regret
  Becomes an April violet,
And buds and blossoms like the rest.

LORD TENNYSON

Spring Goeth all in White

Spring goeth all in white,
Crowned with milk-white may:
In fleecy flocks of light
O'er heaven the white clouds stray:

White butterflies in the air;
White daisies prank the ground:
The cherry and hoary pear
Scatter their snow around.

ROBERT BRIDGES

The Daffodils

I wandered lonely as a cloud
That floats on high o'er vales and hills,
When all at once I saw a crowd,
A host, of golden daffodils;
Beside the lake, beneath the trees,
Fluttering and dancing in the breeze.

Continuous as the stars that shine
And twinkle on the Milky Way,
They stretched in never-ending line
Along the margin of a bay:
Ten thousand saw I at a glance,
Tossing their heads in sprightly dance.

The waves beside them danced, but they
Out-did the sparkling waves in glee:
A poet could not but be gay,
In such a jocund company:
I gazed—and gazed—but little thought
What wealth the show to me had brought:

For oft, when on my couch I lie
In vacant or in pensive mood,
They flash upon that inward eye
Which is the bliss of solitude;
And then my heart with pleasure fills,
And dances with the daffodils.

WILLIAM WORDSWORTH

Pied Beauty

Glory be to God for dappled things—
  For skies of couple-colour as a brinded cow;
    For rose-moles all in stipple upon trout that swim;
Fresh-firecoal chestnut-falls; finches' wings;
  Landscape plotted and pieced—fold, fallow, and plough;
    And all trades, their gear and tackle and trim.

All things counter, original, spare, strange;
  Whatever is fickle, freckled (who knows how?)
    With swift, slow; sweet, sour; adazzle, dim;
He fathers-forth whose beauty is past change:
    Praise him.   GERARD MANLEY HOPKINS

Inversnaid

This darksome burn, horseback brown,
His rollrock highroad roaring down,
In coop and in comb the fleece of his foam
Flutes and low to the lake falls home.

A windpuff-bonnet of fáwn-fróth
Turns and twindles over the broth
Of a pool so pitchblack, féll-frówning,
It rounds and rounds Despair to drowning.

Degged with dew, dappled with dew
Are the groins of the braes that the brook treads through,
Wiry heathpacks, flitches of fern,
And the beadbonny ash that sits over the burn.

What would the world be, once bereft
Of wet and of wildness? Let them be left,
O let them be left, wildness and wet;
Long live the weeds and the wilderness yet.
          GERARD MANLEY HOPKINS

The Thrush's Nest

Within a thick and spreading hawthorn bush,
That overhung a molehill large and round,
I heard from morn to morn a merry thrush
Sing hymns to sunrise, and I drank the sound
With joy; and often, an intruding guest,
I watched her secret toil from day to day,—
How true she warped the moss, to form a nest,
And modelled it within with wood and clay;
And by and by, like heath-bells gilt with dew,
There lay her shining eggs, as bright as flowers,
Ink-spotted-over shells of greeny blue;
And there I witnessed, in the sunny hours
A brood of Nature's minstrels chirp and fly,
Glad as the sunshine and the laughing sky.

JOHN CLARE

The Skylark

The lark, that shuns on lofty boughs to build
Her humble nest, he's silent in the field;
But if (the promise of a cloudless day)
Aurora smiling bids her rise and play,
Then straight she shows 'twas not for want of voice,
Or power to climb, she made so low a choice;
Singing she mounts; her airy wings are stretched
Towards heaven, as if from heaven her notes she fetched.

EDMUND WALLER

The Kingfisher

It was the Rainbow gave thee birth,
    And left thee all her lovely hues;
And, as her mother's name was Tears,
    So runs it in thy blood to choose
For haunts the lonely pools, and keep
In company with trees that weep.

Go you and, with such glorious hues,
   Live with proud Peacocks in green parks;
On lawns as smooth as shining glass,
   Let every feather show its mark;
Get thee on boughs and clap thy wings
Before the windows of proud kings.

Nay, lovely Bird, thou art not vain;
   Thou hast no proud ambitious mind;
I also love a quiet place
   That's green, away from all mankind;
A lonely pool, and let a tree
Sigh with her bosom over me.

W. H. DAVIES

The Linnet

Upon this leafy bush
   With thorns and roses in it,
Flutters a thing of light,
   A twittering linnet,
And all the throbbing world
   Of dew and sun and air
By this small parcel of life
   Is made more fair;
As if each bramble-spray
   And mounded gold-wreathed furze,
Harebell and little thyme,
   Were only hers;
As if this beauty and grace
   Did to one bird belong,
And, at a flutter of wing,
   Might vanish in song.

WALTER DE LA MARE

The Hollow Wood

Out in the sun the goldfinch flits
Along the thistle-tops, flits and twits
Above the hollow wood
Where birds swim like fish—
Fish that laugh and shriek—
To and fro, far below
In the pale hollow wood.

Lichen, ivy, and moss
Keep evergreen the trees
That stand half-flayed and dying,
And the dead trees on their knees
In dog's-mercury and moss:
And the bright twit of the goldfinch drops
Down there as he flits on thistle-tops.

EDWARD THOMAS

The Flycatcher

That is the flycatcher's wing beneath the eaves,
A frivolous quick sound like an opening fan.
Under the scalloped canopy of leaves
He has found the nest made in some other Spring
Between the wall and the tall creeper stem,
Old as the wall itself, a slender tree
(Perhaps one of Raleigh's earliest transplanting);
And now about the window flit from earliest dawn
The skilful wings. A bird of urbane
Elegance is the flycatcher, straight-backed, self-possessed, slim.
He watches and marks his prey and neatly outflies him—
A peregrine in miniature. The midges are conspicuously
Fewer for his hunting.
Good luck, it is said, attends the dwelling that he makes his own.
Certain it is, when he is gone, Summer is gone.

SYLVIA LYND

123

Mallard

Squawking they rise from reeds into the sun,
climbing like furies, running on blood and bone,
with wings like garden shears clipping the misty air,
four mallard, hard winged, with necks like rods
fly in perfect formation over the marsh.

Keeping their distance, gyring, not letting slip the air,
but leaping into it straight like hounds or divers,
they stretch out into the wind and sound their horns again.

Suddenly siding to a bank of air unbidden
by hand signal or morse message of command
downsky they plane, sliding like corks on a current,
designed so deftly that all air is advantage,

till, with few flaps, orderly as they left earth,
alighting among curlew they pad on mud.

REX WARNER

Lapwing

Leaves, summer's coinage spent, golden are all together whirled,
sent spinning, dipping, slipping, shuffled by heavy handed wind,
shifted sideways, sifted, lifted, and in swarms made to fly,
spent sunflies, gorgeous tatters, airdrift, pinions of trees.

Pennons of the autumn wind, flying the same loose flag,
minions of the rush of air, companions of draggled cloud,
tattered, scattered pell mell, diving, with side-slip suddenly wailing
as they scale the uneasy sky flapping the lapwing fly.

Plover, with under the tail pine-red, dead leafwealth in down
    displayed,
crested with glancing crests, sheeny with seagreen, mirror of
    movement
of the deep sea horses plunging, restless, fretted by the whip of wind
tugging green tons, wet waste, lugging a mass to Labrador.

124

See them fall wailing over high hill tops with hue and cry,
like uneasy ghosts slipping in the dishevelled air,
with ever so much of forlorn ocean and wastes of wind
in their elbowing of the air and in their lamentable call.

REX WARNER

Flying Crooked

The butterfly, the cabbage-white,
(His honest idiocy of flight)
Will never now, it is too late,
Master the art of flying straight,
Yet has—who knows so well as I?—
A just sense of how not to fly:
He lurches here and here by guess
And God and hope and hopelessness.
Even the aerobatic swift
Has not his flying-crooked gift.

ROBERT GRAVES

Bat

At evening, sitting on this terrace,
When the sun from the west, beyond Pisa, beyond the mountains of
    Carrara
Departs, and the world is taken by surprise...
When the tired flower of Florence is in gloom beneath the glowing
Brown hills surrounding...
When under the arches of the Ponte Vecchio
A green light enters against stream, flush from the west,
Against the current of obscure Arno...

Look up, and you see things flying
Between the day and the night;
Swallows with spools of dark thread sewing the shadows together.

A circle swoop, and a quick parabola under the bridge arches
Where light pushes through;
A sudden turning upon itself of a thing in the air.
A dip to the water.

125

And you think:
'The swallows are flying so late!'
Swallows?
Dark air-life looping
Yet missing the pure loop...
A twitch, a twitter, an elastic shudder in flight
And serrated wings against the sky,
Like a glove, a black glove thrown up at the light,
And falling back.
Never swallows!
Bats!
The swallows are gone.
At a wavering instant the swallows give way to bats
By the Ponte Vecchio...
Changing guard.
Bats, and an uneasy creeping in one's scalp
As the bats swoop overhead!
Flying madly.
Pipistrello!
Black piper on an infinitesimal pipe.
Little lumps that fly in air and have voices indefinite, wildly vindictive;
Wings like bits of umbrella.
Bats!
Creatures that hang themselves up like an old rag, to sleep;
And disgustingly upside down.
Hanging upside down like rows of disgusting old rags
And grinning in their sleep.
Bats!
In China the bat is symbol of happiness.
Not for me!   D. H. LAWRENCE

Snake

A snake came to my water-trough
On a hot, hot day, and I in pyjamas for the heat,
To drink there.

In the deep, strange-scented shade of the great dark carob-tree
I came down the steps with my pitcher
And must wait, must stand and wait, for there he was at the trough
 before me.

He reached down from a fissure in the earth-wall in the gloom
And trailed his yellow-brown slackness soft-bellied down, over the
 edge of the stone trough
And rested his throat upon the stone bottom,
And where the water had dripped from the tap, in a small clearness,
He sipped with his straight mouth,
Softly drank through his straight gums, into his slack long body,
Silently.

Someone was before me at my water-trough,
And I, like a second comer, waiting.

He lifted his head from his drinking, as cattle do,
And looked at me vaguely, as drinking cattle do,
And flickered his two-forked tongue from his lips, and mused a
 moment,
And stooped and drank a little more,
Being earth-brown, earth-golden from the burning, burning bowels
 of the earth,
On the day of Sicilian July, with Etna smoking.

The voice of my education said to me
He must be killed,
For in Sicily the black, black snakes are innocent, the gold are
 venomous.

And voices in me said, If you were a man
You would take a stick and break him now, and finish him off.
But I must confess how I liked him,
How glad I was he had come like a guest in quiet, to drink at my
 water-trough
And depart peaceful, pacified, and thankless,
Into the burning bowels of this earth.

Was it cowardice, that I dared not kill him?
Was it perversity, that I longed to talk to him?

Was it humility, to feel so honoured?
I felt so honoured.

And yet those voices:
'*If you were not afraid, you would kill him!*'

And truly I was afraid, I was most afraid,
But even so, honoured still more
That he should seek my hospitality
From out the dark door of the secret earth.

He drank enough
And lifted his head, dreamily, as one who has drunken,
And flicked his tongue like a forked night on the air, so black,
Seeming to lick his lips,
And looked around like a god, unseeing, into the air,
And slowly turned his head,
And slowly, very slowly, as if thrice adream,
Proceeded to draw his slow length curving round
And climb again the broken bank of my wall-face.

And as he put his head into that dreadful hole,
And as he slowly drew up, snake-easing his shoulders, and entered
     farther,
A sort of horror, a sort of protest against his withdrawing into that
     horrid black hole,
Deliberately going into the blackness, and slowly drawing himself
     after,
Overcame me now his back was turned.

I looked round, I put down my pitcher,
I picked up a clumsy log
And threw it at the water-trough with a clatter.

I think it did not hit him,
But suddenly that part of him that was left behind convulsed in
     undignified haste,
Writhed like lightning, and was gone
Into the black hole, the earth-lipped fissure in the wall-front,
At which, in the intense still noon, I stared with fascination.

128

And immediately I regretted it.
I thought how paltry, how vulgar, what a mean act!
I despised myself and the voices of my accursed human education.

And I thought of the albatross,
And I wished he would come back, my snake.

For he seemed to me again like a king,
Like a king in exile, uncrowned in the underworld,
Now due to be crowned again.

And so, I missed my chance with one of the lords
Of life.
And I have something to expiate;
A pettiness.   **D. H. LAWRENCE**

Horses on the Camargue

In the grey wastes of dread,
The haunt of shattered gulls where nothing moves
But in a shroud of silence like the dead,
I heard a sudden harmony of hooves,
And, turning, saw afar
A hundred snowy horses unconfined,
The silver runaways of Neptune's car
Racing, spray-curled, like waves before the wind.
Sons of the Mistral, fleet
As him with whose strong gusts they love to flee,
Who shod the flying thunders on their feet
And plunged them with the snortings of the sea;
Theirs is no earthly breed
Who only haunt the verges of the earth
And only on the sea's salt herbage feed—
Surely the great white breakers gave them birth.
For when for years a slave,
A horse of the Camargue, in alien lands,
Should catch some far-off fragrance of the wave
Carried far inland from his native sands,

Camargue] Pampa at the mouth of the Rhône which forms a vast grazing ground for
thousands of wild cattle and horses. [*Author's Note.*]

Many have told the tale
Of how in fury, foaming at the rein,
He hurls his rider; and with lifted tail,
With coal-red eyes and cataracting mane,
Heading his course for home,
Though sixty foreign leagues before him sweep,
Will never rest until he breathes the foam
And hears the native thunder of the deep.
And when the great gusts rise
And lash their anger on these arid coasts,
When the scared gulls career with mournful cries
And whirl across the waste like driven ghosts;
When hail and fire converge
The only souls to which they strike no pain
Are the white-crested fillies of the surge
And the white horses of the windy plain.
Then in their strength and pride
The stallions of the wilderness rejoice;
They feel their Master's trident in their side,
And high and shrill they answer to his voice.
With white tails smoking free,
Long streaming manes, and arching necks, they show
Their kinship to their sisters of the sea—
And forward hurl their thunderbolts of snow.
Still out of hardship bred,
Spirits of power and beauty and delight
Have ever on such frugal pastures fed
And loved to course with tempests through the night.

ROY CAMPBELL

The Pike

From shadows of rich oaks outpeer
The moss-green bastions of the weir,
Where the quick dipper forages
In elver-peopled crevices.
And a small runlet trickling down the sluice
Gossamer music tires not to unloose.

Else round the broad pool's hush
   Nothing stirs.
Unless sometime a straggling heifer crush
Through the thronged spinney where the pheasant whirs;
   Or martins in a flash
Come with wild mirth to dip their magical wings;
While in the shallow some doomed bulrush swings
   At whose hid root the diver vole's teeth gnash.

And nigh this toppling reed, still as the dead
   The great pike lies, the murderous patriarch
   Watching the waterpit shelving and dark,
Where through the plash his lithe bright vassals thread.

      The rose-finned roach and bluish bream
      And staring ruffe steal up the stream
      Hard by their glutted tyrant, now
      Still as a sunken bough.

      He on the sandbank lies,
         Sunning himself long hours
      With stony gorgon eyes:
         Westward the hot sun lowers.

Sudden the gray pike changes, and quivering poises for slaughter;
   Intense terror wakens around him, the shoals scud away, but
      there chances
   A chub unsuspecting: the prowling fins quicken, in fury he
      lances;
And the miller that opens the hatch stands amazed at the whirl in
      the water.   EDMUND BLUNDEN

BALLADS OLD AND NEW

The way in which a ballad tells the story often bears a striking resemblance to the narrative technique of the film.

In both we have a clear directness of action. There is no time lost in details which serve no purpose in forwarding the story.

> The king sits in Dunfermline town
> Drinking the blude-red wine

and we are straight into the tale. Just as the opening shots of a film give us the scene, the characters, and their actions: the small middle-west town, the single street, and the cowboy riding up to the saloon-door.

So with the direct simplicity and economy of the ballad. In one verse we may hear a sailor protesting about the danger of setting out in the face of a coming storm. In the very next verse the ship is already far out to sea:

> They hadna sail'd a league, a league,
> A league but barely three,
> When the lift grew dark, and the wind blew loud,
> And gurly grew the sea.

This is comparable to the quick cutting in the film. We may see a father arguing with his son at the breakfast table and telling him not to fly in bad weather. The next shot shows an aeroplane above the clouds and the son at the controls.

In the ballad there is no criticism, no probing into motives; and the film lets the action and the dialogue tell the story without comment. In both we find a fierce realism—the swift violence of some nursery rhymes and folk-songs—which has

the effect of fantasy. In the film the fights seem incredibly
violent, yet the hurts received belong to a world of make-
believe, so that we are thrilled and excited and not sickened as
we should be if we saw the same violence in real life.

All the details in the ballad are realistic; and it is just this
same realism that makes the film so life-like.

> The cock he hadna craw'd but once
> And clapp'd his wings at a'.

This definiteness is the most striking characteristic of the
ballad, as is the clear reality of the film.

Both use dialogue which is extremely economical. Long
speeches slow down the action in a film where movement is
essential, so film dialogue is terse and pointed, just as in the
ballad.

> 'Where sall we gang and dine today?'

> 'In behint yon auld fail dyke
> I wot there lies a new-slain knight.'

So speak the two ravens.

The ballad makes frequent use of repetition and refrain.
This musical refrain which may be meaningless:

> 'With a hey down down and a down'

has the effect of both hypnotizing and thrilling the audience
—it can lull the audience into a state of ready acceptance and
excite them at the same time—just as film music which can
suddenly spring up from nowhere in the middle of a prairie
(like a meaningless incantation) can lull or excite according to
the action on the screen. Often the repetition is part of the
ballad story:

> O where hae ye been, Lord Randal, my son?
> And where hae ye been, my handsome young man?

and fits in; just as music may be an actual part of the film story (as when someone plays the piano or turns on the gramophone or the radio) when the music, woven into the action, is essential at that point to the mood which it heightens and intensifies. The use of the refrain in the ballad, like the recurrent tune in a film story, may also work up by gradual stages to a climax.

Looked at in this way we may perhaps better appreciate the skill and force of the old ballads, and read them with closer attention and greater enjoyment.

The Laird o' Logie

I will sing, if ye will hearken,
    If ye will hearken unto me;
The King has ta'en a poor prisoner,
    The wanton laird o' young Logie.

Young Logie's laid in Edinburgh chapel;
    Carmichael's the keeper o' the key;
And may Margaret's lamenting sair,
    A' for the love of young Logie.

'Lament, lament na, may Margaret,
    And of your weeping let me be;
For ye maun to the King himsell,
    To seek the life of young Logie.'

May Margaret has kilted her green cleiding,
    And she has curl'd back her yellow hair—
'If I canna get young Logie's life,
    Fareweel to Scotland for evermair.'

When she came before the King,
    She knelit lowly on her knee—
'O what's the matter, may Margaret?
    And what needs a' this courtesie?'

may] maiden.

134

'A boon, a boon, my noble liege,
   A boon, a boon, I beg o' thee!
And the first boon that I come to crave,
   Is to grant me the life of young Logie.'

'O na, O na, may Margaret,
   Forsooth, and so it manna be;
For a' the gowd o' fair Scotland
   Shall not save the life of young Logie.'

But she has stown the King's redding kaim,
   Likewise the Queen her wedding knife,
And sent the tokens to Carmichael,
   To cause young Logie get his life.

She sent him a purse o' the red gowd,
   Another o' the white monie;
She sent him a pistol for each hand,
   And bade him shoot when he gat free.

When he came to the tolbooth stair,
   There he let his volley flee;
It made the King in his chamber start,
   E'en in the bed where he might be.

'Gae out, gae out, my merrymen a',
   And bid Carmichael come speak to me;
For I'll lay my life the pledge o' that,
   That yon's the shot o' young Logie.'

When Carmichael came before the King,
   He fell low down upon his knee;
The very first word that the King spake,
   Was—'Where's the laird of young Logie?'

Carmichael turn'd him round about,
   (I wot the tear blinded his e'e),
'There came a token frae your grace,
   Has ta'en away the laird frae me.'

     redding kaim] dressing comb.   tolbooth] gaol.

'Hast thou play'd me that, Carmichael?
  And hast thou play'd me that?' quoth he;
'The morn the justice court's to stand,
  And Logie's place ye maun supplie.'

Carmichael's awa' to Margaret's bower,
  Even as fast as he may drie—
'O if young Logie be within,
  Tell him to come and speak with me!'

May Margaret turn'd her round about
  (I wot a loud laugh laughed she),
'The egg is chipp'd, the bird is flown,
  Ye'll see nae mair of young Logie.'

The tane is shipped at the pier of Leith,
  The t'other at the Queen's Ferrie:
And she's gotten a father to her bairn,
  The wanton laird of young Logie.

drie] manage.   The tane] The one.

The Gay Goshawk

'O well is me, my gay goshawk,
  That you can speak and flee;
For you can carry a love-letter
  To my true Love from me.'

—'O how can I carry a letter to her?
  Or how should I her know?
I bear a tongue ne'er with her spake,
  And eyes that ne'er her saw.'

—'O well shall ye my true Love ken
  So soon as ye her see:
For of all the flowers of fair England,
  The fairest flower is she.

'And when she goes into the house,
  Sit ye upon the whin;
And sit you there and sing our loves
  As she goes out and in.'

Lord William has written a love-letter,
  Put it under his pinion grey:
And he's awa' to Southern land
  As fast as wings can gae.

And first he sang a low, low note,
  And then he sang a clear;
And aye the o'erword of the sang
  Was 'Your Love can no win here.'

'Feast on, feast on, my maidens all,
  The wine flows you amang;
While I gang to my shot-window
  And hear yon bonnie bird's sang.'

O first he sang a merry sang,
  And then he sang a grave:
And then he peck'd his feathers grey;
  To her the letter gave.

'Have there a letter from Lord William:
  He says, he sent ye three;
He cannot wait your love longer,
  But for your sake he'll die.'

—'I send him the rings from my white fingers,
  The garlands of my hair;
I send him the heart that's in my breast;
  What would my love have mair?
And at Mary's kirk in fair Scotland,
  Ye'll bid him wait for me there.'

whin] gorse-bush.

137

She hied her to her father dear
  As fast as go could she:
'An asking, an asking, my father dear,
  An asking grant you me!
That if I die in fair England,
  In Scotland bury me.

'At the first kirk of fair Scotland,
  You cause the bells be rung;
At the second kirk of fair Scotland,
  You cause the mass be sung;

'And when ye come to Saint Mary's kirk,
  Ye'll tarry there till night.'
And so her father pledged his word,
  And so his promise plight.

The Lady's gone to her chamber
  As fast as she could fare;
And she has drunk a sleepy draught
  That she had mix'd with care.

And pale, pale, grew her rosy cheek,
  And pale and cold was she:—
She seem'd to be as surely dead
  As any corpse could be.

Then spake her cruel stepminnie,
  'Take ye the burning lead,
And drop a drop on her bosom,
  To try if she be dead.'

They dropp'd the hot lead on her cheek,
  They dropp'd it on her chin,
They dropp'd it on her bosom white;
  But she spake none again.

Then up arose her seven brethren,
  And hew'd to her a bier;
They hew'd it from the solid oak;
  Laid it o'er with silver clear.

stepminnie] step-mother.

138

The first Scots kirk that they came to
   They gart the bells be rung;
The next Scots kirk that they came to
   They gart the mass be sung.

But when they came to Saint Mary's kirk,
   There stood spearmen in a row;
And up and started Lord William,
   The chieftain among them a'.

He rent the sheet upon her face
   A little above her chin:
With rosy cheek, and ruby lip,
   She look'd and laugh'd to him.

—'A morsel of your bread, my lord!
   And one glass of your wine!
For I have fasted these three long days
   All for your sake and mine!'

          gart] made.

Johnie of Cocklesmuir

Johnie rose up in a May morning,
   Call'd for water to wash his hands;
And he has call'd for his gude gray hunds,
   That lay bund in iron bands, bands,
   That lay bund in iron bands.

'Ye'll busk, ye'll busk my noble dogs,
   Ye'll busk and mak them boun,
For I'm going to the Broadspear-hill,
   To ding the dun deer doun, doun,
   To ding the dun deer doun.'

Whan Johnie's mither heard o' this,
   She til her son has gane;—
'Ye'll win your mither's benison,
   Gin ye wad stay at hame, hame,
   Gin ye wad stay at hame.

busk] dress.   boun] ready.   ding] beat.   Gin] If.

Your meat sall be of the very, very best,
   And your drink o' the finest wine;
And ye will win your mither's benison,
   Gin ye wad stay at hame, hame,
   Gin ye wad stay at hame.'

His mither's counsel he wad na tak,
   Nor wad he stay at hame;
But he's on to the Broadspear-hill,
   To ding the dun deer doun, doun,
   To ding the dun deer doun.

Johnie lookit east, and Johnie lookit west,
   And a little below the sun;
And there he spied the dun deer sleeping,
   Aneath a buss o' brume, brume,
   Aneath a buss o' brume.

Johnie shot, and the dun deer lap,
   And he's woundit him in the side;
And atween the water and the wud,
   He laid the dun deer's pride, pride,
   He laid the dun deer's pride.

They ate sae meikle o' the venison,
   And drank sae meikle o' the blude,
That Johnie and his twa gray hunds,
   Fell asleep in yonder wud, wud,
   Fell asleep in yonder wud.

By there cam a silly auld man,
   And a silly auld man was he;
And he's aff to the proud foresters,
   To tell what he did see, see,
   To tell what he did see.

'What news, what news, my silly auld man,
   What news, come tell to me?'
'Na news, na news,' said the silly auld man,
   'But what my een did see, see,
   But what my een did see,

     buss o' brume] bush of broom.   lap] sprang.

'As I cam in by yon greenwud,
  And doun amang the scrogs,
The bonniest youth that e'er I saw,
  Lay sleeping atween twa dogs, dogs,
  Lay sleeping atween twa dogs.

'The sark that he had on his back,
  Was o' the Holland sma';
And the coat that he had on his back,
  Was laced wi' gowd fu' braw, braw,
  Was laced wi' gowd fu' braw.'

Up bespak the first forester,
  The first forester of a'—
'An this be Johnie o' Cocklesmuir,
  It's time we were awa, awa,
  It's time we were awa.'

Up bespak the niest forester,
  The niest forester of a'—
'An this be Johnie Cocklesmuir,
  To him we winna draw, draw,
  To him we winna draw.'

The first shot that they did shoot,
  They woundit him on the thie;
Up bespak the uncle's son,—
  'The niest will gar him die, die,
  The niest will gar him die.'

'Stand stout, stand stout, my noble dogs,
  Stand stout and dinna flee;
Stand fast, stand fast, my gude gray hunds,
  And we will mak them die, die,
  And we will mak them die.'

He has killed six o' the proud foresters,
  And wounded the seventh sair;
He laid his leg out owre his steed,
  Says, 'I will kill na mair, mair,'
  Says, 'I will kill na mair.'

scrogs] bushes.   sark] shirt.   braw] fine.   niest] next.   gar] make.

141

Sir Patrick Spens

The king sits in Dunfermline town,
　　Drinking the blude-red wine;
'Oh whare will I get a gude sailor,
　　To sail this ship o' mine?'

Up and spake an eldern knight
　　Sat at the king's right knee;
'Sir Patrick Spens is the best sailor,
　　That ever sail'd the sea.'

The king has written a braid letter,
　　And seal'd it wi' his hand,
And sent it to Sir Patrick Spens,
　　Was walking on the strand.

'To Noroway, to Noroway,
　　To Noroway o'er the faem;
The king's daughter of Noroway,
　　'Tis thou maun bring her hame.'

The first line that Sir Patrick read,
　　A loud laugh laughèd he;
The neist line that Sir Patrick read,
　　The tear blinded his e'e.

'O wha is this has done this deed,
　　And tauld the king o' me,
To send us out at this time o' year,
　　To sail upon the sea?'

'Be't wind, be it weet, be't hail, be it sleet,
　　Our ship must sail the faem,
The king's daughter of Noroway,
　　'Tis we must fetch her hame.'

They hoysed their sails on Monenday morn,
　　Wi' a' the speed they may;
And they hae landed in Noroway,
　　Upon a Wodensday.

They hadna been a week, a week,
  In Noroway, but twae,
When that the lords o' Noroway
  Began aloud to say,

'Ye Scottishmen spend a' our king's goud,
  And a' our queenis fee!'
'Ye lee, ye lee, ye liars loud!
  Fu' loud I hear ye lee!

'For I brought as much white monie,
  As gane my men and me,
And I brought a half-fou o' gude red goud,
  Out o'er the sea wi' me.

'Make ready, make ready, my merry men a'!
  Our gude ship sails the morn.'
'Now, ever alack, my master dear,
  I fear a deadly storm!

'I saw the new moon, late yestreen,
  Wi' the auld moon in her arm;
And if we gang to sea, master,
  I fear we'll come to harm!'

They hadna sail'd a league, a league,
  A league but barely three,
When the lift grew dark, and the wind blew loud,
  And gurly grew the sea.

The ankers brak, and the topmasts lap,
  It was sic a deadly storm;
And the waves came o'er the broken ship,
  Till a' her sides were torn.

'O where will I get a gude sailor,
  To take my helm in hand,
Till I get up to the tall topmast,
  To see if I can spy land?'

gane] would suffice.   lift] sky.   gurly] rough.   lap] sprang.

'O here am I, a sailor gude,
  To take the helm in hand,
Till you go up to the tall topmast,
  But I fear you'll ne'er spy land.'

He hadna gane a step, a step,
  A step but barely ane,
When a bout flew out of our goodly ship,
  And the salt sea it came in.

'Gae, fetch a web o' the silken claith,
  Another o' the twine,
And wap them into our ship's side,
  And let nae the sea come in.'

They fetch'd a web o' the silken claith,
  Another o' the twine,
And they wapp'd them round the gude ship's side,
  But still the sea came in.

O laith, laith were our gude Scots lords
  To wet their cork-heeled shoon!
But lang or a' the play was play'd,
  They wat their hats aboon.

And mony was the feather-bed
  That flattered on the faem;
And mony was the gude lord's son
  That never mair cam hame.

The ladies wrang their fingers white,
  The maidens tore their hair,
A' for the sake of their true loves;
  For them they'll see na mair.

O lang, lang may the ladies sit,
  Wi' their fans into their hand,
Before they see Sir Patrick Spens
  Come sailing to the strand!

bout] bolt.   wap] warp.   flattered] floated.

And lang, lang may the maidens sit,
  Wi' the goud kaims in their hair,
A' waiting for their ain dear loves!
  For them they'll see nae mair.

Half-owre, half-owre to Aberdour,
  'Tis fifty fathoms deep,
And there lies gude Sir Patrick Spens
  Wi' the Scots lords at his feet!

The Wife of Usher's Well

There lived a wife at Usher's Well,
  And a wealthy wife was she;
She had three stout and stalwart sons,
  And sent them o'er the sea.

They hadna been a week from her,
  A week but barely ane,
When word came to the carline wife
  That her three sons were gane.

They hadna been a week from her,
  A week but barely three,
When word came to the carline wife
  That her sons she'd never see.

'I wish the wind may never cease,
  Nor fashes in the flood,
Till my three sons come hame to me,
  In earthly flesh and blood!'

It fell about the Martinmas,
  When nights are lang and mirk,
The carline wife's three sons cam hame,
  And their hats were o' the birk.

ane] one.   carline] aged.   fashes] troubles.   mirk] dark.

It neither grew in syke nor ditch,
　　Nor yet in ony sheugh;
But at the gates o' Paradise,
　　That birk grew fair eneugh.

'Blow up the fire, my maidens!
　　Bring water from the well!
For a' my house shall feast this night,
　　Since my three sons are well.'—

And she has made to them a bed,
　　She's made it large and wide;
And she's ta'en her mantle her about,
　　Sat down at the bedside.

Up then crew the red, red cock,
　　And up and crew the gray;
The eldest to the youngest said,
　　''Tis time we were away.'

The cock he hadna craw'd but once
　　And clapp'd his wings at a',
When the youngest to the eldest said,
　　'Brother, we must awa'.—

The cock doth craw, the day doth daw,
　　The channerin' worm doth chide;
Gin we be miss'd out o' our place,
　　A sair pain we maun bide.'

'Lie still, lie still but a little wee while,
　　Lie still but if we may;
Gin my mother should miss us when she wakes,
　　She'll go mad ere it be day.'

'Fare ye weel, my mother dear!
　　Fareweel to barn and byre!
And fare ye weel, the bonny lass,
　　That kindles my mother's fire!'

syke] marsh.　　sheugh] trench, water-furrow.　　channerin'] complaining, fretting.

The Twa Corbies

As I was walking all alane,
I heard twa corbies making a mane;
The tane unto the t'other did say,
'Where sall we gang and dine to-day?'

'In behint yon auld fail dyke,
I wot there lies a new-slain knight;
And naebody kens that he lies there,
But his hawk, his hound and his lady fair.

'His hound is to the hunting gane,
His hawk to fetch the wild-fowl hame,
His lady's ta'en another mate,
So we may make our dinner sweet.

'Ye'll sit on his white hause-bane,
And I'll pike out his bonny blue een:
Wi' ae lock o' his gowden hair,
We'll theek our nest when it grows bare.

'Mony a one for him makes mane,
But nane sall ken whare he is gane:
O'er his white banes, when they are bare,
The wind sall blaw for evermair.'

corbies] ravens.

Lord Randal

'O where hae ye been, Lord Randal, my son?
And where hae ye been, my handsome young man?'
'I hae been at the greenwood; mother, make my bed soon,
For I'm wearied wi' hunting, and fain wad lie down.'

'An wha met ye there, Lord Randal, my son?
An wha met ye there, my handsome young man?'
'O I met wi' my true-love; mother, make my bed soon,
For I'm wearied wi' hunting, and fain wad lie down.'

'And what did she give you, Lord Randal, my son?
And what did she give you, my handsome young man?'
'Eels fried in a pan; mother, make my bed soon,
For I'm wearied wi' hunting, and fain wad lie down.'

'And wha gat your leavings, Lord Randal, my son?
And wha gat your leavings, my handsome young man?'
'My hawks and my hounds; mother, make my bed soon,
For I'm wearied wi' hunting, and fain wad lie down.'

'And what becam of them, Lord Randal, my son?
And what becam of them, my handsome young man?'
'They stretched their legs out and died; mother, make my bed soon,
For I'm wearied wi' hunting, and fain wad lie down.'

'O I fear you are poisoned, Lord Randal, my son!
I fear you are poisoned, my handsome young man!'
'O yes, I am poisoned; mother, make my bed soon,
For I'm sick at the heart, and I fain wad lie down.'

'What d' ye leave to your mother, Lord Randal, my son?
What d' ye leave to your mother, my handsome young man?'
'Four and twenty milk kine; mother, make my bed soon.
For I'm sick at the heart, and I fain wad lie down.'

'What d' ye leave to your sister, Lord Randal, my son?
What d' ye leave to your sister, my handsome young man?'
'My gold and my silver; mother, make my bed soon,
For I'm sick at the heart, and I fain wad lie down.'

'What d' ye leave to your brother, Lord Randal, my son?
What d' ye leave to your brother, my handsome young man?'
'My houses and my lands; mother, make my bed soon,
For I'm sick at the heart, and I fain wad lie down.'

'What d' ye leave to your true-love, Lord Randal, my son?
What d' ye leave to your true-love, my handsome young man?'
'I leave her hell and fire; mother, make my bed soon,
For I'm sick at the heart, and I fain wad lie down.'

Edward, Edward

'Why does your brand sae drop wi' blude,
        Edward, Edward?
Why does your brand sae drop wi' blude,
    And why sae sad gang ye, O?'
'O I hae kill'd my hawk sae gude,
        Mither, mither;
O I hae kill'd my hawk sae gude,
    And I had nae mair but he, O.'

'Your hawk's blude was never sae red,
        Edward, Edward;
Your hawk's blude was never sae red,
    My dear son, I tell thee, O.'
'O I hae kill'd my red-roan steed,
        Mither, mither;
O I hae kill'd my red-roan steed,
    That erst was sae fair and free, O.'

'Your steed was auld, and ye hae got mair,
        Edward, Edward;
Your steed was auld, and ye hae got mair,
    Some other dule ye dree, O.'
'O I hae kill'd my father dear,
        Mither, mither;
O I hae kill'd my father dear,
    Alas, and wae is me, O!'

'And whatten penance will ye dree for that,
        Edward, Edward?
Whatten penance will ye dree for that?
    My dear son, now tell me, O.'
'I'll set my feet in yonder boat,
        Mither, mither;
I'll set my feet in yonder boat,
    And I'll fare over the sea, O.'

dule ye dree] grief you suffer.

'And what will ye do wi' your tow'rs and your ha',
    Edward, Edward?
And what will ye do wi' your tow'rs and your ha',
  That were sae fair to see, O?'
'I'll let them stand till they doun fa',
    Mither, mither;
I'll let them stand till they doun fa',
  For here never mair maun I be, O.'

'And what will ye leave to your bairns and your wife,
    Edward, Edward?
And what will ye leave to your bairns and your wife
  When ye gang owre the sea, O?'
'The warld's room; let them beg through life;
    Mither, mither;
The warld's room: let them beg through life;
  For them never mair will I see, O.'

'And what will ye leave to your ain mither dear,
    Edward, Edward?
And what will ye leave to your ain mither dear,
  My dear son, now tell me, O?'
'The curse of hell frae me sall ye bear,
    Mither, mither;
The curse of hell frae me sall ye bear,
  Sic counsels ye gave to me, O!'

Helen of Kirconnell

I wish I were where Helen lies;
Night and day on me she cries;
O that I were where Helen lies,
  On fair Kirconnell lea!

Curst be the heart that thought the thought,
And curst the hand that fired the shot,
When in my arms burd Helen dropt,
  And died to succour me!

burd] lady.

O think na ye my heart was sair
When my Love dropt down and spak nae mair!
There did she swoon wi' meikle care
    On fair Kirconnell lea.

As I went down the water-side,
None but my foe to be my guide,
None but my foe to be my guide,
    On fair Kirconnell lea;

I lighted down my sword to draw,
I hackèd him in pieces sma'.
I hackèd him in pieces sma',
    For her sake that died for me.

O Helen fair, beyond compare!
I'll make a garland o' thy hair,
Shall bind my heart for evermair,
    Until the day I dee!

O that I were where Helen lies!
Night and day on me she cries;
Out of my bed she bids me rise,
    Says, 'Haste and come to me!'

O Helen fair! O Helen chaste!
If I were with thee, I were blest,
Where thou lies low and takes thy rest,
    On fair Kirconnell lea.

I wish my grave were growing green,
A winding-sheet drawn owre my een,
And I in Helen's arms lying,
    On fair Kirconnell lea.

I wish I were where Helen lies!
Night and day on me she cries;
And I am weary of the skies,
    For her sake that died for me.

The Greenland Fishery

In seventeen hundred and ninety-four,
  On March the twentieth day;
We hoist our colours to the mast,
  And for Greenland bore away, brave boys!
  And for Greenland bore away.

We were twelve gallant men aboard,
  And to the North did steer:
Old England left we in our wake—
  We sailors knew no fear, brave boys!
  We sailors knew no fear.

Our boatswain to the mast-head went,
  Wi' a spy glass in his hand;
He cries, 'A whale! a whale doth blow,
  She blows at every span, brave boys!
  She blows at every span.'

Our Captain on the master deck
  (A very good man was he),
'Overhaul! overhaul! let the boat tackle fall,
  And launch your boat to sea, brave boys!
  And launch your boat to sea.'

Our boat being launch'd, and all hands in,
  The whale was full in view;
Resolved was then each seaman bold
  To steer where the whale-fish blew, brave boys!
  To steer where the whale-fish blew.

The whale was struck, and the line paid out,
  She gave a flash with her tail;
The boat capsized, and we lost four men
  And we never caught that whale, brave boys!
  And we never caught that whale.

Bad news we to the Captain brought,
The loss of four men true.
A sorrowful man was our Captain then,
And the colours down he drew, brave boys!
And the colours down he drew.

'The losing of this whale,' said he,
'Doth grieve my heart full sore;
But the losing of four gallant men
Doth hurt me ten times more, brave boys!
Doth hurt me ten times more.

'The winter star doth now appear,
So, boys, the anchor weigh;
'Tis time to leave this cold country,
And for England bear away, brave boys!
And for England bear away.

'For Greenland is a barren place,
A land where grows no green,
But ice and snow, and the whale-fish blow,
And the daylight's seldom seen, brave boys!
And the daylight's seldom seen!'

Cawsand Bay

In Cawsand Bay lying, with the Blue Peter flying,
And all hands on deck for the anchor to weigh,
When off came a lady, as fresh as a daisy,
And modestly hailing, the damsel did say:

'Ship ahoy! bear a hand there! I wants a young man there,
So heave us a man-rope, or send him to me;
His name's Henry Grady, and I am a lady,
Arrived to prevent him from going to sea.'

Now the captain, his honour, when he looked upon her,
He ran down the side for to hand her on board.
Cried he, with emotion, 'What son of the ocean
Can thus be looked after by Helena Ford?'

Then the lady made answer, 'That there is a man, sir,
    I'll make him as free as a Duke or a Lord.'—
'Oh no!' says the capp'en, 'That can't very well happen,
    I've got sailing orders—you, sir, stop on board.'

But up spoke the lady, 'Don't you mind him, Hal Grady,
    He once was your capp'en, but now you're at large.
You shan't stop on board her, for all that chap's order!'
    Then out of her bosom she drew his discharge.

Said the captain, 'I'm hang'd now, you're cool, and I'm bang'd now!'
    Said Hal, 'Here, old Weatherface, take all my clothes.'
And ashore then he steer'd her; the lads they all cheer'd her;
    But the captain was jealous, and looked down his nose.

Then she got a shore tailor to rig up her sailor
    In white nankeen trousers and long blue-tail'd coat;
And he looked like a squire, for all to admire,
    With a dimity handkerchief tied round his throat.

They'd a house that was greater than any first-rater,
    With footmen in livery handing the drink,
And a garden to go in, where flowers were blowing,
    The buttercup, daisy, the lily, the pink.

And he got education befitting his station
    (For we all of us know we're not too old to larn);
And his messmates they found him, his little ones round him,
    All chips of the old block from the stem to the starn.

Get Up and Bar the Door

    It fell about the Martinmas time,
        And a gay time it was then,
    When our goodwife got puddings to make,
        And she's boil'd them in the pan.

    The wind sae cauld blew south and north,
        And blew into the floor:
    Quoth our goodman, to our goodwife,
        'Gae out and bar the door.'

'My hand is in my hussy'fskap,
　Goodman, as ye may see,
An it shou'd nae be barr'd this hundred year,
　It's no be barr'd for me.'

They made a paction 'tween them twa,
　They made it firm and sure;
That the first word whae'er shou'd speak,
　Shou'd rise and bar the door.

Then by there came two gentlemen,
　At twelve o'clock at night,
And they could neither see house nor hall,
　Nor coal nor candle light.

'Now, whether is this a rich man's house,
　Or whether is it a poor?'
But ne'er a word wad ane o' them speak,
　For barring of the door.

And first they ate the white puddings,
　And then they ate the black;
Tho' muckle thought the goodwife to hersel',
　Yet ne'er a word she spake.

Then said the one unto the other,
　'Here, man, tak ye my knife,
Do ye tak aff the auld man's beard,
　And I'll kiss the goodwife.'

'But there's nae water in the house,
　And what shall we do than?'
'What ails ye at the pudding broo,
　That boils into the pan?'

O up then started our goodman,
　An angry man was he;
'Will ye kiss my wife before my een,
　And sca'd me wi' pudding bree?'

155

Then up and started our goodwife,
    Gied three skips on the floor;
'Goodman, you've spoken the foremost word,
    Get up and bar the door.'

Casey Jones

Come all you rounders if you want to hear
The story of a brave engineer;
Casey Jones was the hogger's name,
On a big eight-wheeler, boys, he won his fame.
Caller called Casey at half-past four,
He kissed his wife at the station door,
Mounted to the cabin with orders in his hand,
And took his farewell trip to the promised land.

    Casey Jones, he mounted to the cabin,
    Casey Jones, with his orders in his hand!
    Casey Jones, he mounted to the cabin,
    Took his farewell trip into the promised land.

Put in your water and shovel in your coal,
Put your head out the window, watch the drivers roll,
I'll run her till she leaves the rail,
'Cause we're eight hours late with the Western Mail!
He looked at his watch and his watch was slow,
Looked at the water and the water was low,
Turned to his fireboy and said,
'We'll get to 'Frisco, but we'll all be dead!'
                                    (*Refrain*)

Casey pulled up Reno Hill,
Tooted for the crossing like a whippoorwill,
Snakes all knew by the engine's moans
That the hogger at the throttle was Casey Jones.
He pulled up short two miles from the place,
Number Four stared him right in the face,
Turned to his fireboy, said, 'You'd better jump,
'Cause there's two locomotives that's going to bump!'
                                    (*Refrain*)

Casey said, just before he died,
'There's two more roads I'd like to ride.'
Fireboy said, 'What can they be?'
'The Aitchison-Topeka and the Santa Fé.'
Mrs Jones sat on her bed a-sighing,
Got a pink that Casey was dying,
Said, 'Go to bed, children; hush your crying,
'Cause you'll get another papa on the Salt Lake line.'

> Casey Jones! Got another papa!
> Casey Jones, on the Salt Lake Line!
> Casey Jones! Got another papa!
> Got another papa on the Salt Lake Line.

Jock of Hazeldean

'Why weep ye by the tide, ladie?
  Why weep ye by the tide?
I'll wed ye to my youngest son,
  And ye sall be his bride:
And ye sall be his bride, ladie,
  Sae comely to be seen'—
But ay she loot the tears down fa'
  For Jock of Hazeldean.

'Now let this wilfu' grief be done,
  And dry that cheek so pale;
Young Frank is chief of Errington,
  And lord of Langley-dale;
His step is first in peaceful ha',
  His sword in battle keen'—
But ay she loot the tears down fa'
  For Jock of Hazeldean.

'A chain of gold ye sall not lack,
  Nor braid to bind your hair,
Nor mettled hound, nor managed hawk,
  Nor palfrey fresh and fair;

And you, the foremost o' them a',
   Shall ride our forest queen'—
But ay she loot the tears down fa'
   For Jock of Hazeldean.

The kirk was deck'd at morning-tide,
   The tapers glimmer'd fair;
The priest and bridegroom wait the bride,
   And dame and knight are there.
They sought her baith by bower and ha';
   The ladie was not seen!
She's o'er the Border, and awa'
   Wi' Jock of Hazeldean.

SIR WALTER SCOTT

Lochinvar

O, young Lochinvar is come out of the west,
Through all the wide Border his steed was the best;
And save his good broadsword he weapons had none;
He rode all unarm'd, and he rode all alone.
So faithful in love, and so dauntless in war,
There never was knight like the young Lochinvar.

He stayed not for brake, and he stopp'd not for stone,
He swam the Esk river where ford there was none;
But ere he alighted at Netherby gate
The bride had consented, the gallant came late:
For a laggard in love, and a dastard in war,
Was to wed the fair Ellen of brave Lochinvar.

So boldly he enter'd the Netherby Hall,
Among bride's-men, and kinsmen, and brothers, and all:
Then spoke the bride's father, his hand on his sword
(For the poor craven bridegroom said never a word),
'O come ye in peace here, or come ye in war,
Or to dance at our bridal, young Lord Lochinvar?'—

'I long woo'd your daughter, my suit you denied;—
Love swells like the Solway, but ebbs like its tide—
And now am I come, with this lost love of mine,
To lead but one measure, drink one cup of wine.
There are maidens in Scotland more lovely by far,
That would gladly be bride to the young Lochinvar.'

The bride kiss'd the goblet; the knight took it up,
He quaff'd off the wine, and he threw down the cup,
She look'd down to blush, and she look'd up to sigh,
With a smile on her lips, and a tear in her eye.
He took her soft hand, ere her mother could bar,—
'Now tread we a measure!' said young Lochinvar.

So stately his form, and so lovely her face,
That never a hall such a galliard did grace;
While her mother did fret, and her father did fume,
And the bridegroom stood dangling his bonnet and plume;
And the bride-maidens whisper'd, ''Twere better by far,
To have match'd our fair cousin with young Lochinvar.'

One touch to her hand, and one word in her ear,
When they reach'd the hall-door, and the charger stood near;
So light to the croupe the fair lady he swung,
So light to the saddle before her he sprung!
'She is won! we are gone, over bank, bush, and scaur;
They'll have fleet steeds that follow,' quoth young Lochinvar.

There was mounting 'mong Graemes of the Netherby clan;
Forsters, Fenwicks, and Musgraves, they rode and they ran:
There was racing and chasing, on Cannobie Lee,
But the lost bride of Netherby ne'er did they see.
So daring in love, and so dauntless in war,
Have ye e'er heard of gallant like young Lochinvar?

SIR WALTER SCOTT

Lord Ullin's Daughter

A Chieftain to the Highlands bound
  Cries 'Boatman, do not tarry!
And I'll give thee a silver pound
  To row us o'er the ferry!'

'Now who be ye, would cross Lochgyle
  This dark and stormy water?'
'O I'm the chief of Ulva's isle,
  And this, Lord Ullin's daughter.

'And fast before her father's men
  Three days we've fled together,
For should he find us in the glen,
  My blood would stain the heather.

'His horsemen hard behind us ride—
  Should they our steps discover,
Then who will cheer my bonny bride
  When they have slain her lover?'

Out spoke the hardy Highland wight,
  'I'll go, my chief, I'm ready:
It is not for your silver bright,
  But for your winsome lady:—

'And by my word! the bonny bird
  In danger shall not tarry;
So though the waves are raging white
  I'll row you o'er the ferry.'

By this the storm grew loud apace,
  The water-wraith was shrieking;
And in the scowl of heaven each face
  Grew dark as they were speaking.

But still as wilder blew the wind
  And as the night grew drearer,
Adown the glen rode armèd men,
  Their trampling sounded nearer.

'O haste thee, haste!' the lady cries,
  'Though tempests round us gather;
I'll meet the raging of the skies,
  But not an angry father.'

The boat has left a stormy land,
  A stormy sea before her,—
When, oh! too strong for human hand
  The tempest gathered o'er her.

And still they rowed amidst the roar
  Of waters fast prevailing:
Lord Ullin reached that fatal shore,—
  His wrath was changed to wailing.

For, sore dismayed, through storm and shade
  His child he did discover:—
One lovely hand she stretched for aid,
  And one was round her lover.

'Come back! come back!' he cried in grief,
  'Across this stormy water:
And I'll forgive your Highland chief,
  My daughter!—O my daughter!'

'Twas vain: the loud waves lashed the shore,
  Return or aid preventing:
The waters wild went o'er his child,
  And he was left lamenting.

                    THOMAS CAMPBELL

Henry Hudson's Voyage

The Queen of Westminster declared,
Declared, and drove him forth:
'The Kingdom of old Tartary
Lies somewhere to the north.'

The merchant men they scolded him—
He, trapped inside the Bay,
Who failed to find across the Pole
A passage to Cathay.

He has forgotten them; they came
Plump, trooping to the quay,
Beruffed, befurred, the shrewd, the wise
Muscovy Company.

Gone are the rowing-men in red,
The splashing and the cries,
The palaces, the luminous
Dove-light of Greenwich skies;

Above, above, on cliffs of ice
Set sheer above the bay,
He sees them, golden at the last,
The Cities of Cathay.

What visions and what memories rise
To damn him, or console,
Who falls asleep, who dies within
The circle of the Pole?

His eyelids have worn thin, and seem
Transparent to his eyes,
Only the colour of the North
Distracts the night he dies.

Only the gulping seas, pressed up
Through fissures of the floes,
Only the cannonade of ice
Makes music when he goes.

Only the bergs, like flames afloat,
Tower tapering to the light;
Charge on, and grind, and swing apart,
Spinning in copper night.

Above, above, on cliffs of ice
Set sheer above the bay,
He sees them, golden at the last,
The Cities of Cathay.

DOROTHY WELLESLEY

The Ballad of the Brides of Quair

A stillness crept about the house,
At evenfall, in noon-tide glare;
Upon the silent hills looked forth
The many-windowed House of Quair.

The peacock on the terrace screamed;
Browsed on the lawn the timid hare;
The great trees grew i' the avenue,
Calm by the sheltered House of Quair.

The pool was still; around its brim
The alders sickened all the air;
There came no murmur from the streams,
Though nigh flowed Leithen, Tweed, and Quair.

The days hold on their wonted pace,
And men to court and camp repair,
Their part to fill, of good or ill,
While women keep the House of Quair.

And one is clad in widow's weeds,
And one is maiden-like and fair,
And day by day they seek the paths
About the lonely fields of Quair.

To see the trout leap in the streams,
The summer clouds reflected there,
The maiden loves in pensive dreams
To hang o'er silver Tweed and Quair.

Within, in pall-black velvet clad,
Sits stately in her oaken chair—
A stately dame of ancient name—
The Mother of the House of Quair.

Her daughter broiders by her side,
With heavy drooping golden hair,
And listens to her frequent plaint,—
'Ill fare the Brides that come to Quair.

'For more than one hath lived in pine,
And more than one hath died of care,
And more than one hath sorely sinned,
Left lonely in the House of Quair.

'Alas! and ere thy father died
I had not in his heart a share,
And now—may God forfend her ill—
Thy brother brings his Bride to Quair!'

She came: they kissed her in the hall,
They kissed her on the winding stair,
They led her to her chamber high,
The fairest in the House of Quair.

They bade her from the window look,
And mark the scene how passing fair,
Among whose ways the quiet days
Would linger o'er the wife of Quair.

''Tis fair,' she said on looking forth,
'But what although 'twere bleak and bare'—
She looked the love she did not speak,
And broke the ancient curse of Quair—

'Where'er he dwells, where'er he goes,
His dangers and his toils I share.'
What need be said—she was not one
Of the ill-fated Brides of Quair!

ISA CRAIG KNOX

Croker of Ballinagarde

Ballinagarde was a house to be sure
With windows that went from the ceiling to floor,
And fish in the river and hens in the yard
And Croker was master of Ballinagarde.

There were mares in the meadows: the grass was so good
The cows never tired of chewing the cud;
One mouthful sufficed all the sheep on the sward;
They forced them to fatten at Ballinagarde.

So close and convenient and wide were his grounds
He could hunt with the Tipps or the Waterford hounds;
And many's the cup and the Horse Show award
That shone on the sideboard in Ballinagarde.

He bought his own whiskey but brewed his own ale
That foamed up like beastings that thicken the pail.
No fiddler no more than the man with his card
Was ever sent empty from Ballinagarde.

His daughter got married at sweet twenty-two:
To lose her was more than her father could do.
To give her away it had gone very hard,
You could see that by Croker of Ballinagarde.

The wedding was over a week and a day
Before the last guest could be driven away;
For everyone's going he tried to retard:
'What ails ye?' cried Croker of Ballinagarde.

One day when out hunting and going like fire
His horse was flung down—Oh, bad Scrant to the wire!
And something in Croker was broken or marred,
So the parson was sent for to Ballinagarde.

The parson remarked as the grounds he drove through
'The land's in good heart. What a beautiful view!
It's but what I'm thinking 'twill go very hard
To comfort the owner of Ballinagarde.'

He tried to persuade him and make him resigned,
On Heavenly mansions to fasten his mind.
'There's a Land that is fairer than this,' he declared.
'I doubt it!' said Croker of Ballinagarde.

O. ST J. GOGARTY

The Goose

I knew an old wife lean and poor,
　　Her rags scarce held together;
There strode a stranger to the door,
　　And it was windy weather.

He held a goose upon his arm,
　　He uttered rhyme and reason,
'Here, take the goose, and keep you warm,
　　It is a stormy season.'

She caught the white goose by the leg,
　　A goose—'twas no great matter.
The goose let fall a golden egg
　　With cackle and with clatter.

She dropped the goose, and caught the pelf,
　　And ran to tell her neighbours;
And blessed herself, and cursed herself,
　　And rested from her labours.

And feeding high, and living soft,
　　Grew plump and able-bodied;
Until the grave churchwarden doffed,
　　The parson smirked and nodded.

So sitting, served by man and maid,
　　She felt her heart grow prouder:
But ah! the more the white goose laid
　　It clacked and cackled louder.

It cluttered here, it chuckled there
　　It stirred the old wife's mettle:
She shifted in her elbow-chair,
　　And hurled the pan and kettle.

'A quinsy choke thy cursèd note!'
　　Then waxed her anger stronger.
'Go, take the goose, and wring her throat,
　　I will not bear it longer.'

Then yelped the cur, and yawled the cat;
   Ran Gaffer, stumbled Gammer.
The goose flew this way and flew that,
   And filled the house with clamour.

As head and heels upon the floor
   They floundered all together,
There strode a stranger to the door,
   And it was windy weather:

He took the goose upon his arm,
   He uttered words of scorning;
'So keep you cold, or keep you warm,
   It is a stormy morning.'

The wild wind rang from park and plain,
   And round the attics rumbled,
Till all the tables danced again,
   And half the chimneys tumbled.

The glass blew in, the fire blew out,
   The blast was hard and harder.
Her cap blew off, her gown blew up,
   And a whirlwind cleared the larder;

And while on all sides breaking loose
   Her household fled the danger,
Quoth she, 'The Devil take the goose,
   And God forget the stranger!'

LORD TENNYSON

The Rider at the Gate

A windy night was blowing on Rome,
The cressets guttered on Caesar's home,
The fish-boats, moored at the bridge, were breaking
The rush of the river to yellow foam.

167

The hinges whined to the shutters shaking,
When clip-clop-clep came a horse-hoof raking
The stones of the road at Caesar's gate;
The spear-butts jarred at the guard's awaking.

'Who goes there?' said the guard at the gate.
'What is the news, that you ride so late?'
'News most pressing, that must be spoken
To Caesar alone, and that cannot wait.'

'The Caesar sleeps: you must show a token
That the news suffice that he be awoken.
What is the news, and whence do you come?
For no light cause may his sleep be broken.'

'Out of the dark of the sands I come,
From the dark of death, with news for Rome.
A word so fell that it must be uttered
Though it strike the soul of Caesar dumb.'

Caesar turned in his bed and muttered,
With a struggle for breath the lamp-flame guttered;
Calpurnia heard her husband moan:
    'The house is falling,
The beaten men come into their own.'

'Speak your word,' said the guard at the gate;
'Yes, but bear it to Caesar straight,
Say, "Your murderer's knives are honing,
Your killer's gang is lying in wait."

'Out of the wind that is blowing and moaning,
Through the city palace and the country loaning,
I cry, "For the world's sake, Caesar, beware,
And take this warning as my atoning.

'"Beware of the Court, of the palace stair,
Of the downcast friend who speaks so fair,
Keep from the Senate, for Death is going
On many men's feet to meet you there.

loaning] field.

168

'"I, who am dead, have ways of knowing
Of the crop of death that the quick are sowing.
I, who was Pompey, cry it aloud
From the dark of death, from the wind blowing.

'"I, who was Pompey, once was proud,
Now I lie in the sand without a shroud;
I cry to Caesar out of my pain,
Caesar, beware, your death is vowed."'

The light grew grey on the window-pane,
The windcocks swung in a burst of rain,
The window of Caesar flung unshuttered,
The horse-hoofs died into wind again.

Caesar turned in his bed and muttered,
With a struggle for breath the lamp-flame guttered;
Calpurnia heard her husband moan:
        'The house is falling,
The beaten men come into their own.'

                                  JOHN MASEFIELD

Heriot's Ford

'What's that that hirples at my side?'—
    'The foe that you must fight, my Lord.'
'That rides as fast as I can ride?'—
    'The shadow of your might, my Lord.'

'Then wheel my horse against the foe!'—
    'He's down and overpast, my Lord.
You war against the sunset glow:
    The judgment follows fast, my Lord.'

'Oh, who will stay the sun's descent?'—
    'King Joshua, he is dead, my Lord.'
'I need an hour to repent!'—
    ''Tis what our sister said, my Lord.'

169

'Oh do not slay me in my sins!'—
   'You're safe awhile with us, my Lord.'
'Nay, kill me ere my fear begins!'—
   'We would not serve you thus, my Lord.'

'Where is the doom that I must face?'—
   'Three little leagues away, my Lord.'
'Then mend the horses' laggard pace!'—
   'We need them for next day, my Lord.'

'Next day, next day! Unloose my cords!'—
   'Our sister needed none, my Lord.
You had no mind to face our swords,
   And—where can cowards run, my Lord?'

'You would not kill the soul alive?'—
   ''Twas thus our sister cried, my Lord.'
'I dare not die with none to shrive.'—
   'But so our sister died, my Lord.'

'Then wipe the sweat from brow and cheek.'—
   'It runnels forth afresh, my Lord.'
'Uphold me, for the flesh is weak.'—
   'You've finished with the flesh, my Lord.'

                    RUDYARD KIPLING

O What is that Sound

O what is that sound which so thrills the ear
   Down in the valley drumming, drumming?
Only the scarlet soldiers, dear,
   The soldiers coming.

O what is that light I see flashing so clear
   Over the distance brightly, brightly?
Only the sun on their weapons, dear,
   As they step lightly.

O what are they doing with all that gear;
    What are they doing this morning, this morning?
Only the usual manœuvres, dear,
    Or perhaps a warning.

O why have they left the road down there;
    Why are they suddenly wheeling, wheeling?
Perhaps a change in the orders, dear;
    Why are you kneeling?

O haven't they stopped for the doctor's care;
    Haven't they reined their horses, their horses?
Why, they are none of them wounded, dear,
    None of these forces.

O is it the parson they want with white hair;
    Is it the parson, is it, is it?
No, they are passing his gateway, dear,
    Without a visit.

O it must be the farmer who lives so near;
    It must be the farmer so cunning, so cunning?
They have passed the farm already, dear,
    And now they are running.

O where are you going? stay with me here!
    Were the vows you swore me deceiving, deceiving?
No, I promised to love you, dear,
    But I must be leaving.

O it's broken the lock and splintered the door,
    O it's the gate where they're turning, turning;
Their boots are heavy on the floor
    And their eyes are burning.

W. H. AUDEN

THE POET'S HEART

Our earliest feelings are those centred round some simple object such as a doll or a toy train, a dog or a pet rabbit. As we grow older we extend our feelings from our personal possessions to our home, our friends, our school and our country. These feelings become settled because of the value to us of what they stand for. We like to be with our friends because we enjoy their company; we play games, go for picnics, have enjoyable times together. Feelings bound up with something instinctive, the desire for company, and with an enduring idea such as that of friendship, are called sentiments.

> I will gather and carefully make my friends
> Of the men of the Sussex Weald,
> They watch the stars from silent folds,
> They stiffly plough the field,
> By them and the God of the South Country
> My poor soul shall be healed.

Poets often express sentiments when they write about a beautiful scene:

> Earth has not anything to show more fair:
> Dull would he be of soul who could pass by
> A sight so touching in its majesty.

Such a feeling may turn to a love of one's own country, and the poet might cry:

> This is my own, my native land!

and utter patriotic sentiments such as:

> We're the sons of sires that baffled
> Crowned and mitred tyranny

or

> We must be free or die, who speak the tongue
> That Shakespeare spake; the faith and morals hold
> Which Milton held.

Poems expressing such sentiments quicken and enlarge our sympathies, and we come to admire courage, endurance, and self-sacrifice when we read:

> Here and here did England help me: how can I help England

and we can be uplifted by the vigorous expression of man's enduring spirit:

> Strong in will
> To strive, to seek, to find, and not to yield.

Adlestrop

Yes. I remember Adlestrop—
The name, because one afternoon
Of heat the express-train drew up there
Unwontedly. It was late June.

The steam hissed. Some one cleared his throat.
No one left and no one came
On the bare platform. What I saw
Was Adlestrop—only the name

And willows, willow-herb, and grass,
And meadowsweet, and haycocks dry,
No whit less still and lonely fair
Than the high cloudlets in the sky.

And for that minute a blackbird sang
Close by, and round him, mistier,
Farther and farther, all the birds
Of Oxfordshire and Gloucestershire.

EDWARD THOMAS

Upon Westminster Bridge

Earth has not anything to show more fair:
Dull would he be of soul who could pass by
A sight so touching in its majesty:
This City now doth like a garment wear
The beauty of the morning; silent, bare,
Ships, towers, domes, theatres, and temples lie
Open unto the fields, and to the sky;
All bright and glittering in the smokeless air.
Never did sun more beautifully steep
In his first splendour, valley, rock, or hill
Ne'er saw I, never felt, a calm so deep!
The river glideth at his own sweet will:
Dear God! the very houses seem asleep;
And all that mighty heart is lying still!

WILLIAM WORDSWORTH

The South Country

When I am living in the Midlands
    That are sodden and unkind,
I light my lamp in the evening:
    My work is left behind;
And the great hills of the South Country
    Come back into my mind.

The great hills of the South Country
    They stand along the sea;
And it's there walking in the high woods
    That I could wish to be,
And the men that were boys when I was a boy
    Walking along with me.

The men that live in North England
    I saw them for a day:
Their hearts are set upon the waste fells,
    Their skies are fast and grey;

From their castle-walls a man may see
  The mountains far away.

The men that live in West England
  They see the Severn strong,
A-rolling on rough water brown
  Light aspen leaves along.
They have the secret of the Rocks,
  And the oldest kind of song.

But the men that live in the South Country
  Are the kindest and most wise,
They get their laughter from the loud surf,
  And the faith in their happy eyes
Comes surely from our Sister the Spring
  When over the sea she flies;
The violets suddenly bloom at her feet,
  She blesses us with surprise.

I never get between the pines
  But I smell the Sussex air;
Nor I never come on a belt of sand
  But my home is there.
And along the sky the line of the Downs
  So noble and so bare.

A lost thing could I never find,
  Nor a broken thing mend:
And I fear I shall be all alone
  When I get towards the end.
Who will there be to comfort me
  Or who will be my friend?

I will gather and carefully make my friends
  Of the men of the Sussex Weald,
They watch the stars from silent folds,
  They stiffly plough the field.
By them and the God of the South Country
  My poor soul shall be healed.

If I ever become a rich man,
    Or if ever I grow to be old,
I will build a house with deep thatch
    To shelter me from the cold,
And there shall the Sussex songs be sung
    And the story of Sussex told.

I will hold my house in the high wood
    Within a walk of the sea,
And the men that were boys when I was a boy
    Shall sit and drink with me.

HILAIRE BELLOC

You That Love England

You that love England, who have an ear for her music,
The slow movement of clouds in benediction,
Clear arias of light thrilling over her uplands,
Over the chords of summer sustained peacefully;
Ceaseless the leaves' counterpoint in a west wind lively,
Blossom and river rippling loveliest allegro,
And the storms of wood strings brass at year's finale:
Listen. Can you not hear the entrance of a new theme?

You who go out alone, on tandem or on pillion,
Down arterial roads riding in April,
Or sad beside lakes where hill-slopes are reflected
Making fires of leaves, your high hopes fallen:
Cyclists and hikers in company, day excursionists,
Refugees from cursed towns and devastated areas;
Know you seek a new world, a saviour to establish
Long-lost kinship and restore the blood's fulfilment.

You who like peace, good sticks, happy in a small way
Watching birds or playing cricket with schoolboys,
Who pay for drinks all round, whom disaster chose not;
Yet passing derelict mills and barns roof-rent

Where despair has burnt itself out—hearts at a standstill,
Who suffer loss, aware of lowered vitality;
We can tell you a secret, offer a tonic; only
Submit to the visiting angel, the strange new healer.

You above all who have come to the far end, victims
Of a run-down machine, who can bear it no longer;
Whether in easy chairs chafing at impotence
Or against hunger, bullies and spies preserving
The nerve for action, the spark of indignation—
Need fight in the dark no more, you know your enemies.
You shall be leaders when zero hour is signalled,
Wielders of power and welders of a new world.

C. DAY LEWIS

Patriotism

Breathes there the man with soul so dead,
Who never to himself hath said,
  'This is my own, my native land!'
Whose heart hath ne'er within him burn'd
As home his footsteps he hath turn'd
  From wandering on a foreign strand?

SIR WALTER SCOTT

Home-thoughts, from the Sea

Nobly, nobly Cape Saint Vincent to the North-west died away;
Sunset ran, one glorious blood-red, reeking into Cadiz Bay;
Bluish 'mid the burning water, full in face Trafalgar lay;
In the dimmest North-east distance dawn'd Gibraltar grand and
    gray;
'Here and here did England help me: how can I help England?'—
    say,
Whoso turns as I, this evening, turn to God to praise and pray,
While Jove's planet rises yonder, silent over Africa.

ROBERT BROWNING

The Soldier

If I should die, think only this of me:
   That there's some corner of a foreign field
That is for ever England. There shall be
   In that rich earth a richer dust concealed;
A dust whom England bore, shaped, made aware,
   Gave, once, her flowers to love, her ways to roam,
A body of England's, breathing English air,
   Washed by the rivers, blest by suns of home.

And think, this heart, all evil shed away,
   A pulse in the eternal mind, no less
      Gives somewhere back the thoughts by England given;
Her sights and sounds; dreams happy as her day;
   And laughter, learnt of friends; and gentleness,
      In hearts at peace, under an English heaven.

RUPERT BROOKE

The Volunteer

Here lies the clerk who half his life had spent
Toiling at ledgers in a city grey,
Thinking that so his days would drift away
With no lance broken in life's tournament:
Yet ever 'twixt the books and his bright eyes
The gleaming eagles of the legions came,
And horsemen, charging under phantom skies,
Went thundering past beneath the oriflamme.

And now those waiting dreams are satisfied;
From twilight to the halls of dawn he went;
His lance is broken; but he lies content
With that high hour, in which he lived and died
And falling thus, he wants no recompense,
Who found his battle in the last resort;
Nor needs he any hearse to bear him hence,
Who goes to join the men of Agincourt.

HERBERT ASQUITH

How Sleep the Brave

How sleep the brave, who sink to rest
By all their country's wishes blest!
When Spring, with dewy fingers cold,
Returns to deck their hallow'd mould,
She there shall dress a sweeter sod
Than Fancy's feet have ever trod.

By fairy hands their knell is rung;
By forms unseen their dirge is sung;
There Honour comes, a pilgrim grey,
To bless the turf that wraps their clay;
And Freedom shall awhile repair
To dwell, a weeping hermit, there!

                                    WILLIAM COLLINS

Men of England

Men of England! who inherit
    Rights that cost your sires their blood!
Men whose undegenerate spirit
    Has been proved on land and flood

By the foes ye've fought, uncounted,
    By the glorious deeds ye've done,
Trophies captured—breaches mounted,
    Navies conquered—kingdoms won!

Yet, remember, England gathers
    Hence but fruitless wreaths of fame,
If the freedom of your fathers
    Glow not in your hearts the same.

What are monuments of bravery,
    Where no public virtues bloom?
What avail in lands of slavery
    Trophied temples, arch, and tomb?

Pageants!—Let the world revere us
   For our people's rights and laws,
And the breasts of civic heroes
   Bared in Freedom's holy cause.

Yours are Hampden's, Russell's glory,
   Sydney's matchless shade is yours,—
Martyrs in heroic story
   Worth a hundred Agincourts!

We're the sons of sires that baffled
   Crowned and mitred tyranny:—
They defied the field and scaffold
   For their birthrights—so will we!
             THOMAS CAMPBELL

It is not to be thought of that the flood

It is not to be thought of that the flood
Of British freedom, which, to the open sea
Of the world's praise, from dark antiquity
Hath flowed, 'with pomp of waters, unwithstood,'—
Roused though it be full often to a mood
Which spurns the check of salutary bands,—
That this most famous stream in bogs and sands
Should perish; and to evil and to good
Be lost for ever. In our halls is hung
Armoury of the invincible Knights of old:
We must be free or die, who speak the tongue
That Shakespeare spake; the faith and morals hold
Which Milton held.—In everything we are sprung
Of Earth's first blood, have titles manifold.
             WILLIAM WORDSWORTH

Jerusalem

And did those feet in ancient time
   Walk upon England's mountains green?
And was the holy Lamb of God
   On England's pleasant pastures seen?

And did the Countenance Divine
   Shine forth upon our clouded hills?
And was Jerusalem builded here
   Among these dark Satanic Mills?

Bring me my bow of burning gold!
   Bring me my arrows of desire!
Bring me my spear! O clouds, unfold!
   Bring me my chariot of fire!

I will not cease from mental fight,
   Nor shall my sword sleep in my hand,
Till we have built Jerusalem
   In England's green and pleasant land.

              WILLIAM BLAKE

I love all beauteous things

I love all beauteous things,
   I seek and adore them;
God hath no better praise,
And man in his hasty days
   Is honoured for them.

I too will something make
   And joy in the making;
Altho' to-morrow it seem
Like the empty words of a dream
   Remembered on waking.

             ROBERT BRIDGE

There was an Indian

There was an Indian, who had known no change,
   Who strayed content along a sunlit beach
Gathering shells. He heard a sudden strange
   Commingled noise: looked up; and gasped for speech.

For in the bay, where nothing was before,
    Moved on the sea, by magic, huge canoes,
With bellying cloths on poles, and not one oar,
    And fluttering coloured signs and clambering crews.

And he, in fear, this naked man alone,
    His fallen hands forgetting all their shells,
His lips gone pale, knelt low behind a stone,
    And stared, and saw, and did not understand,
Columbus's doom-burdened caravels
    Slant to the shore, and all their seamen land.

                             J. C. SQUIRE

On first looking into Chapman's Homer

Much have I travelled in the realms of gold,
    And many goodly states and kingdoms seen;
    Round many western islands have I been
Which bards in fealty to Apollo hold.
Oft of one wide expanse had I been told,
    That deep-browed Homer ruled as his demesne:
    Yet did I never breathe its pure serene
Till I heard Chapman speak out loud and bold:
Then felt I like some watcher of the skies
    When a new planet swims into his ken;
Or like stout Cortez, when with eagle eyes
    He stared at the Pacific—and all his men
 Looked at each other with a wild surmise—
    Silent, upon a peak in Darien.   JOHN KEATS

Bermudas

Where the remote Bermudas ride
In the ocean's bosom unespied,
From a small boat that row'd along
The listening winds received this song:

'What should we do but sing His praise
That led us through the watery maze
Unto an isle so long unknown,
And yet far kinder than our own?
Where He the huge sea-monsters wracks,
That lift the deep upon their backs,
He lands us on a grassy stage,
Safe from the storms' and prelates' rage:
He gave us this eternal Spring
Which here enamels everything,
And sends the fowls to us in care
On daily visits through the air:
He hangs in shades the orange bright
Like golden lamps in a green night,
And does in the pomegranates 'close
Jewels more rich than Ormuz shows:
He makes the figs our mouths to meet
And throws the melons at our feet;
But apples plants of such a price,
No tree could ever bear them twice.
With cedars chosen by His hand
From Lebanon He stores the land;
And makes the hollow seas that roar
Proclaim the ambergris on shore.
He cast (of which we rather boast)
The Gospel's pearl upon our coast;
And in these rocks for us did frame
A temple where to sound His name.
Oh, let our voice His praise exalt
Till it arrive at Heaven's vault,
Which thence (perhaps) rebounding may
Echo beyond the Mexique bay!'

Thus sung they in the English boat
A holy and a cheerful note:
And all the way, to guide their chime,
With falling oars they kept the time.

ANDREW MARVELL

183

Ulysses

It little profits that an idle king,
By this still hearth, among these barren crags,
Matched with an aged wife, I mete and dole
Unequal laws unto a savage race,
That hoard, and sleep, and feed, and know not me.
I cannot rest from travel: I will drink
Life to the lees; all times I have enjoyed
Greatly, have suffered greatly, both with those
That loved me, and alone; on shore, and when
Through scudding drifts the rainy Hyades
Vext the dim sea; I am become a name;
For always roaming with a hungry heart
Much have I seen and known; cities of men
And manners, climates, councils, governments
Myself not least, but honoured of them all;
And drunk delight of battle with my peers,
Far on the ringing plains of windy Troy.
I am a part of all that I have met;
Yet all experience is an arch wherethrough
Gleams that untravelled world, whose margin fades
For ever and for ever when I move.
How dull it is to pause, to make an end,
To rust unburnished, not to shine in use!
As though to breathe were life. Life piled on life
Were all too little, and of one to me
Little remains; but every hour is saved
From that eternal silence, something more,
A bringer of new things; and vile it were
For some three suns to store and hoard myself,
And this grey spirit yearning in desire
To follow knowledge like a sinking star,
Beyond the utmost bound of human thought.

This is my son, mine own Telemachus,
To whom I leave the sceptre and the isle—
Well-loved of me, discerning to fulfil
This labour, by slow prudence to make mild

A rugged people, and through soft degrees
Subdue them to the useful and the good.
Most blameless is he, centred in the sphere
Of common duties, decent not to fail
In offices of tenderness, and pay
Meet adoration to my household gods,
When I am gone. He works his work, I mine.

There lies the port; the vessel puffs her sail:
There gloom the dark broad seas. My mariners,
Souls that have toiled, and wrought, and thought with me—
That ever with a frolic welcome took
The thunder and the sunshine, and opposed
Free hearts, free foreheads—you and I are old;
Old age hath yet his honour and his toil;
Death closes all; but something ere the end,
Some work of noble note, may yet be done,
Not unbecoming men that strove with Gods.
The lights begin to twinkle from the rocks:
The long day wanes: the slow moon climbs: the deep
Moans round with many voices. Come, my friends,
'Tis not too late to seek a newer world.
Push off, and sitting well in order smite
The sounding furrows; for my purpose holds
To sail beyond the sunset, and the baths
Of all the western stars, until I die.
It may be that the gulfs will wash us down:
It may be we shall touch the Happy Isles,
And see the great Achilles, whom we knew.

Though much is taken, much abides; and though
We are not now that strength which in old days
Moved earth and heaven; that which we are, we are;
One equal temper of heroic hearts,
Made weak by time and fate, but strong in will
To strive, to seek, to find, and not to yield.

                                        LORD TENNYSON

INDEX OF AUTHORS

INDEX OF AUTHORS

INDEX OF FIRST LINES

INDEX OF FIRST LINES